HALF A CENTURY AGO

ANGELA ARIAS

This memoir narrates the lived experiences of a young immigrant girl in New York City during the 1970s.

Fulton Books
Meadville, PA

Published by Fulton Books 2024

ISBN 979-8-88982-259-2 (paperback)
ISBN 979-8-88982-260-8 (digital)

Printed in the United States of America

I don't study to know more, but to ignore less.

—Sor Juana Inés de la Cruz

Beyond myself, somewhere,
I wait for my arrival.

—Octavio Paz

Elsewhere is a conscious choice to remain
in the incomplete. Your elsewhere is no
one else's, but it's the same in its fragile
liminality. We live in a suspension bridge,
and some days windier than others.

—Elamin Abdelmahmoud

For my daughter Elena Kilcullen

ACKNOWLEDGEMENTS

I would like to thank:
My late father, Angel Arias, for giving me his name and providing me with unconditional love, guidance, and support.

My mother, Andrea Arias, for being the source of strength in our family.

My sisters Yolanda and Ody, who provided many of the instances that made my memories real.

My brother Angel for sharing my name and making us laugh all the time at the dinner table.

The many friends and other family members who encouraged me to pursue my passion for writing.

Marcia, Jessie, Nancy, Bob, Betty, Ms. Forte, Yuri, Michelle, Ana Rosa and her late father Yamil, my neighbor Lee, my students for allowing me to keep my memories alive, and the team at the Advanced class at Sarah Lawrence College Writing Institute.

PROLOGUE

At home, the dinner table was the place to share all types of stories about everyone's daily whereabouts and happenings. It provided the place and created the moments in time when my parents shared anecdotes about life issues that impacted the ways in which they wanted to raise their four children amid an ever changing and hostile world. We were newcomers in a land that did not always welcome us, but in which we continuously attempted to overcome the strife and hardship faced daily both at school and at work.

In this memoir, I attempt to recollect the long-ago memories of the child who arrived in the Bronx, New York, in 1971 with an inquisitive mind and a yearning for learning about life. The memories of a loving family and parents who were intentional about raising children who would someday become fruitful members of society are still present in my memory even now, half a century later.

Fifty years later, my siblings and I continue to provide opportunities for gathering around a dinner table and telling stories about each other's lives. The affection and respect that my parents instilled in us as young children continues to permeate our relationships despite growing up and forming our own paths away from each other.

JULY 20, 1971

In the darkness amid a tropical night, I lay wide-awake with feelings of anticipation of the events of the day to follow. "Buzz," mosquitoes disturbed my ear. Cows in the distance made their usual noise, and birds flapping their wings as they moved about the side of the farmhouse. In the adjacent bedroom, *Abuelo* (grandpa) snored on and on. *Abuela* (grandma) coughed her usual loud raspy sound. The sweat dripped on the side of my temples, pasting my curls to the back of my neck. I spent most nights leading up to this glorious day awake and feeling butterflies in my stomach.

Over and over, I imagined the reunification with my parents, who were faraway in New York. There were visions in my mind of tall buildings and many people going about the streets as I had seen in movies. My eyes were wide open when the first day light seeped through the cracks of the windowpanes. The roosters had been cackling for a while, and the usual neighing of the farm horses had all announced dawn for this new day. It was July 20.

For the past three months, my siblings and I lived at my paternal grandparents' farmhouse, where they were the oldest members of our large extended family. The big farm accommodated a group of multigenerational people who lived there on a regular basis, while others came and went according to harvest season. My siblings and I were there in passing, awaiting to leave for the United States.

It had been exactly two years and a month since my parents left my siblings and I behind in our homeland. My parents left on a plane to New York City. "We will soon send for you," they told my younger two sisters, my brother, and me, "when we are able to secure a home in the new land." I was the oldest of my siblings, and before leaving the Dominican Republic, "Take care of your younger siblings," my mom told me. "Be a good role model to them," she said several times before leaving. My parents left us behind under the care of my grandparents, Aunt Isabel, and the nuns at a boarding school. I had yet to turn nine years old when my parents left us under their care in June of 1969.

My parents' departure created a lot of disruption to our way of life. My little sister was too young for school and remained with my aunt and grandparents in a valley town in the countryside of the province of Baní. My sister Loli, my brother Angel, and I went to our old coastal hometown called Boca Chica at a boarding school with nuns. The school was about a three-hour drive from my grandparents' town.

The first weeks without my parents were hard on all of us because we missed our parents' constant hugs and kisses. The nuns were very cold to all the children at the school. My siblings and I often hugged each other just because. "Estamos solos," I reminded them every time. My soul felt empty, and it was scary to realize my parents were so far away, *lejos*. They were so far that it was hard for me to conceptualize the distance. My imagination placed them on the other side of the world, and when I looked at a blinking star, thoughts that they were staring at it as well created butterflies in my stomach. I winked at the blinking star and imagined my dad winking back and whispering to me about his whereabouts, "Aquí estoy."

My night prayers for the well-being of my parents became a source of daily consolation for me. "Dear God, *Diosito…*," I began my prayers so they would soon be able to send for my siblings and me. My greatest fear was that they would die in New York and never be able to return nor send for us, as they'd promised. Whenever I read the newspaper, following the racial riots of the 1960s in the United States, I was scared that my parents would be hurt amid all the chaos in the country they now called home.

At that time, there was also social grief in our homeland, leftover from the US intervention, which locals called the invasion of 1965. At home, there was also a corrupt government which made life difficult for most citizens. Remnants of that chaotic time lingered in my memory from time to time. My awareness of social ills led me to dedicate a large part of my life to assisting the disenfranchised populations of society working as an educator.

My abuelo used to say that government officials were corrupt and that they needed many prayers. "They are looters," said Abuelo whenever I inquired about the people in charge. "Someday you will understand. Go play now, little one," he rushed me off when I insisted on asking questions he deemed too advanced for my age.

My young age was not an obstacle for me to understand social issues because I read the newspaper for my maternal grandmother since age 5. Reading the news for others to hear was one of my daily duties as the oldest child in my immediate family. While living at the farm with my paternal grandparents, again I became a designated reader for other elderly people who were unable to read. Most afternoons after the siesta, I would sit under the *jabillo* tree, and several neighbors would sit around sipping coffee or lemonade as I read the news to them. That tree provided a nice protection from the sun during very sunny days. Its big branches extended wide and created a natural umbrella. Its leaves were wide and fanned themselves with the wind. I enjoyed dramatizing some events, and my favorite type of news were those about political and social issues.

When I was not reading the newspaper, my favorite readings were storybooks. They provided a safe place for me. I imagined becoming a time traveler and a life warrior with various superpowers and healing qualities. My father left behind a wooden trunk full of classic books. For the three months in the farm, I read most of Dante's *Divine Comedy* and Cervantes's *Don Quixote de la Mancha* while sitting up high on the jabillo tree. Up above, there was a comfortable landing made by three thick branches, and I used to sit in the middle and read for hours as the tropical breeze kept me comfortable up there.

While immersed in a book during a very hot day, I fell asleep on the landing of the jabillo tree. A lot of commotion below woke me up, and I heard my siblings and cousins calling out my name,

"Angelita, dónde estás?"

When I looked down and let them know I was up there, they told me that they had spent hours searching for me all over the farm.

"We found her, Abuela!" they said while jumping up and down. My abuela was very worried that something awful happened to me somewhere in the vast farm. From that day on, whenever Abuela needed me, she sent one of the kids to look for me up on the landing in the jabillo tree.

*****

On July 20, 1971, as daylight began to seep through the window, I got up as soon as I heard my Abuelo shuffle his *chancleta* (house sandals) around toward the back of the house. My grandparents slept in the room adjacent to the one assigned to my siblings and me. Every morning at the crack of dawn, I heard my abuelo wake up and get ready for his duties at the farm. Abuela followed him soon after and went into the kitchen area to light up the coffeepot. The farmhouse was large, with several bedrooms and other side structures attached to the main building.

Abuelo was old but had the strength of a mule and was wise as an eagle. That's what I heard some of my older cousins say about Abuelo. The mules used to carry the heavy crops brought back from the large farm. He owned the most land in town and was "the most respected man around," they also said. People came from all around to ask for his advice and guidance, and many listened to his words of wisdom as he spoke slowly and thoughtfully in a soft and tender low voice. I enjoyed watching Abuelo from afar as he whispered tenderly to the honeybees after returning from his big farm that was far away. The bees never seemed to bother him and often landed on his shoulders and arms when he pulled out the various compartments in his small apiary on the back side of the big house.

This morning in July, when I stood up from bed after hearing Abuelo get up, a sense of sadness invaded my gut when the sudden realization hit me that I would be separating from my grandparents while joining my parents overseas. A feeling of deep sadness invaded my heart when I caught up with them in the kitchen.

"Bendición," I greeted them in the kitchen, while hugging Abuelo's arm as he blessed my forehead with the sign of the cross. The cool touch of his skin against my forehead and the smell of mangoes that emanated from his neatly pressed weekend shirt felt very familiar to me.

"So you and your siblings leave us today to catch up with your parents in New York," he said. "Remember to learn good English so you can become a good *oficinista*, office professional," he added, looking down at me with a half smile as I continued to hug his arm. "Also remember to always honor our name with good deeds," Abuelo concluded as he hugged me back.

That morning, as we got ready to leave my grandparents' home for the airport, many cousins and aunts and uncles came to say good-bye. Several of them had tears in their eyes when they hugged us and brought gifts to take to my parents abroad. Most of the gifts were left behind because we could not fit them all into our limited luggage.

My mother had sent a letter a few weeks before with specific instructions as to what we were to bring with us. Almost all our belongings were donated to needy people in town. My mother said in her letter that she had purchased all new clothes and toys for us, so we needed not to bring but a few essentials.

That morning, so many people came in and out of my grandparents' ranch that it was almost impossible to know how many hugs and kisses we had received. "The bus is here," someone yelled. A bus arrived midmorning and parked in front of the house.

"Why a bus?" I asked my older cousin Nena, who was brushing my hair. Later, I discovered that many people would travel to the airport to see us off.

The usual cousins who lived around the ranch and many other people gave us a sendoff. "No se olviden de nosotros." Many of my cousins kept reminding us not to forget them and said how much they wished they could also come along with us.

At some point in time, Abuelo announced that it was almost time to leave for the airport and that the bus was ready and so was my uncle's car. My grandparents rode in the car with my little sister Ody, and the rest of the people loaded the bus that Abuelo rented.

The bus ride to the airport was eventful and fun. First, we were led in prayer by my tia Isabel. The rest of the time, we sang popular songs and made-up ones the entire way to the airport. One of the cousins brought along his guitar and played it most of the way.

The bus began its course past the farmland onto the towns along the way to the capital city, Santo Domingo, and after through the towns leading toward the airport. The road toward the airport was very familiar to me since it was the same path to our former hometown before my parents left for the United States.

When the bus turned onto the road that led to the airport, I closed my eyes to feel the breeze from the ocean as it tickled my cheeks and made my hair curly. I could almost taste the salt as I took a gulp of air and held the breeze in my mouth.

Once we arrived at the airport, there was a fast pace to the process for departure. On the walk to the departure gate, my tia Isabel carried my little sister Ody and held tight to my brother's hand. I held on to my abuelo's hand, and my sister Loli was cared for by my abuela, and as they both walked arm in arm, they cried the entire time we walked to the gate. Abuela walked side by side to my nine-year-old sister, and I noticed that they were the same height.

Every bone in my body shook with excitement as we approached the gate, and I could feel Abuelo trying to calm me down. "No tengas miedo," he said a few times, and gazed down at me while holding my hand tighter.

Walking next to Abuelo made me feel safe and minimized my fear of the unfamiliar life ahead. My younger siblings and I were about to board a plane for the first time and fly along the Atlantic Ocean north to meet with my parents after more than two years of separation. We were boarding a plane full of strangers, and the only people we knew were each other. Years later, when I left home for college, feelings of separation and fear of the unknown were already posited in my heart.

When I asked Abuelo how many people would be on the plane, he said about one hundred. That seemed like a lot of people to me, but he reassured me that everything would be all right. "Todo va a estar bien, el piloto sabe lo que hace." He also stated that the pilot knew his job well, and he would fly the big metal bird smoothly like an expert. I trusted he was correct about the plane ride.

The traveling cousins, a nice older woman and her young adult son, who were to care for us during our flight, had our paperwork and passports inside a plastic folder, and they answered the questions posed by immigration officials. The cousins became annoyed when they discovered Loli and I had mangoes in our handbags.

"You can't bring those with you," they scolded us as they discarded them. My tia Isabel sent two mangoes for my dad because he had been away the longest, and that was his favorite fruit. I could not understand why that would be a problem if we had it in our bags. In the handbags my aunt crafted for us, she had placed a few pieces of hard candy, a little pack of gum, an embroidered handkerchief, and a small mango from Abuelo's backyard.

My knees were shaking when we reached the departure gate, down a long hallway. We received yet another set of hugs and kisses from the elders in the family. "Que Dios los bendiga mis hijos," were the last words we heard from our family as we left the homeland, the Dominican Republic. When I looked back one more time, they were all waving goodbye and blowing kisses in the air.

We traveled on Pan Am Airlines. The flight crew dressed in meticulous blue-and-white uniforms. The ladies wore a small hat above their pulled-up hair, and white gloves. The air inside the plane was chilly, and it smelled like new furniture. The flight attendant helped accommodate my sister Ody's seat and food tray. I watched her and did the same to get ready to eat. "Enjoy your meal," she said softly as she passed the trays.

During the flight, my heart was pounding so feverishly that I could hear it in my ears, and my entire body trembled with excitement. I had envisioned this moment so many times, and now that it was finally time to travel, I did not know what to do with myself. One moment my legs were crossed; the next second, my hands were pressed between my back and the seat. At one point, I caught myself biting my nails. I was just so fidgety during that flight.

After four hours in the air, our stewardess, the voice of perfection, made the landing announcement. She spoke both in Spanish and English and said to get ready for landing at JFK International Airport in New York City.

The steps down the airplane and the long hallway to the immigration processing section seemed endless. I had never walked down such long hallways nor seen so many people lined up anywhere. The anticipation of reuniting with my parents weighed heavily on me as I longed to finally embrace them.

The immigration building was frigid. There was an unfamiliar smell that was void of ocean air and the smell of fresh fruit. The railing up the second level stairs was blistering cold. The escalator moved slowly as people waved through the tinted glass as they reached the last step.

Announcements in what I assumed were other languages were being made constantly and bright lights illuminated the place and made it feel as if we were inside a big television set. The bright lights made my eyes squint, and I blinked wildly. A big welcoming sign on the front wall of the escalator greeted everyone.

When we got to the immigration booth, the agent asked each one of us for our names. Because I was the oldest, he confirmed with me that we were there to reunite with my parents who lived in New York City and that the adults traveling with us were cousins who were only taking care of us during the flight.

"Vienen ustedes para reunir con sus padres?" he said, trying to verify we were meeting with our parents. His Spanish sounded different from other adults back home. I assumed that he was an American who spoke Spanish only for his job. He tried to smile, but never parted his lips to do so. "Tienen frutas?" he asked me. Now I understood why the cousins had made us leave the mangoes we were bringing for my dad.

After the immigration booth, we were guided by the traveling cousins to walk down another long hallway to collect our luggage. My siblings and I shared one suitcase and a small matching blue handbag. The luggage came out a rotating belt with all other suitcases, many of which looked similar. We recognized our blue suitcase and matching smaller bag as soon as it came out.

The traveling cousins told us to look through the smoky glass to spot my parents. "Búsquenlos," they said. They were anxious to let us go so they could move on with their plans.

Luckily, my parents were waiting with open arms as we walked out of the gate. Papi was on his knees and hugged us all at once. He was crying with joy. Mami was also bawling. My sister Loli, my brother Angel, and Ody were all shedding tears. My uncle Ramon, who came along with my parents to greet us, used a handkerchief for his eyes. I guess that I was also teary, but I do not remember. I do recall shaking, elated, and jumping up and down as I rubbed my hands against my blue dress.

It was great to finally be reunited with my parents in New York City. It had been two years and a month since we separated and had not seen our dad. Our mom went to visit us after one year and spent a week before returning to work in New York. It was a hot and humid walk to the car at the parking garage. We were so happy to be together again. Papi led the way to the parked car, and we hummed to songs like *"Caballito blanco,"* and hopped our way to the car as if we were each riding an imaginary horse. Mami and her brother watched and smiled as they followed us in a hurried pace. Hugging my parents again was better than I had imagined. I had longed for this day since they left.

Glancing out the car window was fascinating to me. There were roads that connected and intertwined all along the way. "Wow!" my siblings and I said every time we noticed something new. We pointed out that the tall buildings looked like boxes with little holes for windows. "That view in the distance is the city of New York with many skyscrapers," pointed out Papi when I inquired.

"When will we visit the big city?" we asked.

We went into some underpasses on the road. I closed my eyes in fear when we went under a train rail. I had never seen train rails in the air. Sections of the roads were being repaired, so the ride was bumpy and reminded me of the roads in the countryside at Abuelo's hometown. Growing up in New York City, I continued to make comparisons between the world I left behind and my new reality.

The air in New York City had an unfamiliar smell of something burning in the distance, as well as stinky garbage. On that July 20, 1971, I had woken up in the tropics with the scent of mangoes and fresh earth and traveled to another country in North America where there was no sea breeze and no salty taste to the air, but a putrid gust of garbage and metallic smoke. As we continued to drive toward our new home, dusk began to fall upon New York City.

FIRST BIRTHDAY IN
THE NEW LAND

A week had passed since arriving at our new home in New York City. Every day seemed like new opportunities and ways to do things, and events were being unveiled in front of my eyes. Life's reality of life was challenging, but we were all together again as a family of six. So it was truly a thrilling ride.

We ate together at the dinner table in a small corner of the living room at the same time every day, and it became our moment to share stories about the two years we spent separated from each other. Our parents listened attentively to our tales about the boarding school and later about Abuelo's farm.

Most nights, I was often woken up by the loud sound of sirens passing by our street. There was constant noise that was invasive to my ears and which scared me out of my sleep. In the distance, there was an intermittent smell of burning wood and metal that tickled my throat and made me cough incessantly. I was not really used to all the pollution thrown at me.

That morning, because the smell of fire was so prominent, I approached the window and looked around but did not see spot any smoke anywhere around. It was the beginning of the day, and the sun had barely risen. There were only a few cars passing by, but there were people waiting at the bus stop across the street. Each person carried a small bag, and some had tools in their hands. There was a man smoking, and he was not carrying anything and kept his spare hand in his pocket. He paced up and down the street as if he needed a bathroom. One of the ladies held a black book covered like the one Mami had for her Bible. I assumed the people at the bus stop were heading to work.

That day was my eleventh birthday, and it had been seven days since my siblings and I reunited with our parents. Living in a very small apartment on the fourth floor of a loud and very smelly neighborhood was not easy. It was a huge adjustment for us all.

"We are finally together," said my parents often as they caressed anyone of us. "We have waited for the opportunity to bring you with us as we promised when we left," they said. "Enthusiasm and love is all we can offer you for now," said Papi one day as he explained that this was only the beginning to a path to many accomplishments ahead.

We lived in a cramped apartment. The largest room in the apartment became the kids' bedroom, where my parents had crammed four little beds lined up against each corner of the room. There were two tiny dressers and scarce items in the small closet. The walls smelled of fresh paint, and there was a compact fan perched on one of the windows. There was a minute kitchen with no room to walk about. The pots were shiny, and the expresso coffeepot was always on the stove. That was also very shiny. It was interesting to me that there was brightly colored yellow paper on the kitchen walls. When I asked Mami why there was paper on the wall, she shrugged her shoulders. "We found the kitchen like this when we moved in. I scrubbed it down and made it shiny," she explained.

Mami had taken the week off from work to care for us while we got used to the new home. Over that week, she had instructed us to not open the door to anyone, to never put our heads out the windows, don't jump nor step too hard since there were neighbors who lived downstairs, to avoid making too much noise as not to disturb the old lady next door. Among a list of other things not to do were screaming, leaving toys around, playing or eating on the beds, wetting the bathroom floor when we showered, and many more rules I do not remember anymore. Rules were always important to Mami.

That first week, Mami also gave my sister Loli and me a list of chores for which we were responsible. We were responsible for all the house chores. She had instructed us how to do each task and watched over us as we struggled to learn them. My brother Angel and my sister Ody were spared of any further responsibilities other than caring for their toys because they were younger.

That first week we were also introduced to a whole new set of extended family members. Papi had cousins who helped him settle in when my parents arrived two years earlier. Our parents told us that we should treat them with respect and be forever grateful for their support. The elder of the cousins would take care of us when Mami returned to work after our first week in the Bronx. Mrs. Rosa worked from home, sewing for a garment factory, and she would keep an eye on us while Mami worked. Later, she would pick us up from school when school began. She was a sweet lady who seemed as old as my grandparents. Mrs. Rosa had wrinkles on her neck just like my abuela had. Her hands shook when she threaded her machine, and she wore small glasses at the tip of her nose when she needed to focus.

That morning, I don't know how long I had been staring out the window but never noticed when Papi came into the room whistling a happy birthday song. He picked me up from where I had been sitting on my bed by the window and hugged me dearly, wishing me the happiest of birthdays. He went on chanting his favorite song to me:

"Angelita / flor bonita / pedazo de melancolía / yo te quiero niña linda / cada noche / cada día." (Angie / my melancholic pretty flower / I love you, pretty girl / every day and every night).

Most days Papi would recite these words to me as if to reassure his love for his firstborn. Hearing these words again made me very happy. I smiled from ear to ear every time he chanted them. That day was super special since it was my first birthday on US soil.

While Papi was making a big fuss over me, my siblings woke up, and they all hopped on my bed to tell stories with my dad. Papi was an easygoing and jolly man who loved to laugh and give us hugs. He also kissed us every time he entered a room. Papi expressed his joy that we were all together again. "I am very happy and thankful to God that my children are with me again," he said these words very often during our first week reunited. While we were having a grand old time, Mami walked into the room to announce, "El desayuno está listo." And off we ran to have breakfast before Papi needed to hurry up and get ready for work. "I asked permission to arrive late this morning," he said.

Papi worked long hours six days a week. I watched him take the bus across the street every morning. He also carried the little bag that Mami gave him with his lunch. He stood at the bus stop with the rest of the people who were all holding little bags as well. Papi left every morning by six in the morning and returned home after seven in the evening. Upon returning from work, he always said he had a good day when asked and often told us funny stories about people he encountered at work or on his way there. "If you had seen what happened today on the bus," and he would tell us a story that made us all laugh. Papi always saw the good side of life and appreciated the most minuscule of moments about everyday living.

Earlier that week, Mami had brought us to a different park on the Grand Concourse where rows of gray-haired people sat on benches. It was not possible for us to play there since we were yelled at when a ball got too close to one of the old ladies sitting on a bench. We begged Mami not to take us to that park again. We nicknamed it *"parque de viejitos"* because of the amount of elderly people who often went there. At this new park, although we were not ready for the pool that day since we had no swimsuits, we had lots of fun playing and running around.

That afternoon, on my birthday, Mami took us to the park. It had swings, areas for racket ball, basketball hoops, sprinkles, and a pool. We nicknamed it "the kids' fun park." At the new park, we felt very comfortable since there were many kids and activities to enjoy.

"Ay, Dios mio!" Mami screamed when Angel got into the sprinklers and got all wet. We had spent almost a week inside our small apartment, and my brother especially was full of energy to be released. Angel ran around the entire time we were there. He wanted to climb on trees, on the fence that separated the basketball courts from the rest of the area and ran in and around the sprinklers until he was totally drenched.

"Ay!" Loli fell from a swing and scraped her knee. She cried, and Mami washed the blood off her wound with water from the water fountain in the park. She continued to play after Mami caressed her head and blew on her injured knee.

Ody made new friends at the park. "Look at me!" she gleefully yelled across the way. She was always easygoing when making new friends. She was a jolly six-year-old with a big smile that exposed her outward-shaped two front teeth. The kids her age seemed to understand each other although they did not speak much.

I enjoyed going on the swing, and when Mami was not looking, I tried standing on it as the big girls were doing. "Yippee!" I yelled when I was able to push myself up high on the swing. I remember thinking that someday I hoped to master the skill standing on the big swing and propelling myself high up in the air. I liked heights and loved the feeling of observing things from above, like a bird in flight.

That evening Papi returned from work with a big smile and carrying a box and a bouquet of flowers for me. I missed getting flowers on my last two birthdays. Papi always brought flowers when it was any of our birthdays. He brought flowers for my mom every Saturday since they had been engaged in 1958. Until shortly before he passed away in 2016, I remember my father had continued to bring flowers for my mother every week, even at times when he could barely afford them. When he became ill with dementia at the end of his life, either my sister Loli or I would bring flowers so he could give them to our mother.

That night, we enjoyed dinner as a family and improvised a little birthday party for me afterward. The box Papi brought with him had a present for me. I received my first sewing machine. It was a toy machine, but it allowed me to sew small pieces of fabric with it.

"Let's dance," said Papi while pulling Mami to the middle of the living room and spinning her around. He loved music and had several LPs he had collected since coming to New York. We all danced to merengue, and Papi began to teach us how to dance to new music, and for the first time, I was introduced to salsa. He told us that salsa music was a Latino dance from the Bronx, which is where we lived. "For most songs, the lyric tells a story and are often derived from a poem," he said. "Un, dos, trés." He clapped his hands with the beat, and "one, two, three," we mimicked him.

Daddy also taught us several words in English that week. He pronounced the word *Bronx* with a heavy intonation on the first two letters "Brr…," and we mimicked him along the other words he would tell us during our first week as immigrants. Every evening since we had been here turned into a language and culture lesson for us. Papi would show us how to say certain words both in English and in Spanish. "Words must be used grammatically correct. Intonation is a different thing," Papi would often say. He was very particular about proper language use.

When home, Mami spent most of the day cleaning and cooking and teaching us about manners and acceptable behavior. Using forks and a knife properly was important to her, along with washing up and dressing for dinner. "Get your elbows off the table," she often said. "Stand up straight," she told me as she poked my back when I slouched. She claimed we had lost much of our decorum since she had to leave us behind in the Dominican Republic.

It was a very good feeling to have our family finally together for a celebration. That night, as I prayed in my bed to thank God for the fortune of having my parents and my siblings, I was delighted that we were all together again. It made me very glad that my parents had been able to keep their promise to send for us. It also made me happy that they were never hurt during any of the fires in the Bronx, nor during the social protests that continued to happen in the city. I was ecstatic that they both had jobs to be able to sustain us. I was very joyful that on that day. I was eleven years old.

SUMMER OF '71

The summer in New York was very hot and humid. We spent most of the time in our apartment or at the apartment of our elderly cousins who took care of us while our parents went to work. Every morning, our parents woke up before sunrise so my dad could travel to Queens to work at a factory where the pieces of coats would be precut to be sent off to another factory where the sewing would take place. My dad would come home at the end of the day just before dusk after taking two trains and a bus. He always walked in with a smile, and on his way up the four flights to our apartment on the fourth floor, we heard him whistle a tune every day. Papi would pick each one of us up in the air and kiss and hug each one with his favorite phrase because he had a particular rhyme for each child. The phrase for me was "Angelita, flor bonita [Angie, beautiful flower]."

Every evening, by the time my dad came home, Mami had already picked us up from the cousins' house and had already cooked dinner. She worked at a pen factory in the South Bronx. Mami came home very tired every day, and I could see her vein sticking out on her left temple. Her legs were often swollen, but she hardly complained about her ailments. Mami said that only weak people complained all the time, and she was not about to tolerate having a complaint department at home. Loli and I took turns placing warm towels on Mami's legs the few times she sat with us to watch TV after dinner. Mami cooked our meals every day, and she sighed in silence as she moved quickly about the kitchen. She insisted on setting the table with clean linen every night. She wanted to continue the old traditions we had in our old country. My sister, Loli, and I took care of setting the table properly and cleaning the dishes immediately after dinner. Every night, before we went to bed, the kitchen was shiny as new. Mami would inspect that and the bathroom as if she were a supervisor at one of those factories where she had worked since she came to this country. She did not smile much but was very loving. We always waited for our dad so we could eat together.

We looked forward to the weekend. Mami was off from work both days, and Papi came home earlier on Saturdays and was off on Sunday. Every Saturday afternoon, we went to the park with Mami. We hopped on the merry-go-round and onto the swings, then to the sprinkler if it was a hot sunny day. One Saturday in early August, Mami took us shopping for swimwear. We were finally equipped for the pool. Mami enjoyed the pool most since she was an avid swimmer. She had lived by the ocean all her life before coming to New York and often told us stories about her swimming days as a kid in her hometown, Barahona.

Every Sunday, after church, my parents took us for a tour of the city. We rode the subway from Yankee Stadium stop to various destinations in Manhattan. That first summer my family visited many of the historical landmarks in NYC. The day we went to the Statue of Liberty, only my mother climbed with us up the spiral stairway to the top. My dad was afraid of heights. He stayed behind, holding our bag with snacks and other things my mom insisted we carried everywhere we went. Through a little window at the top, I was able to see very far. Across a body of water, which I later learned was the bay of New York, I could see a town with rusted buildings and on the other side the longest bridge I could have imagined. It was a clear day, so the horizon seemed very far away. At the tip south of the island of Manhattan, there were the skeletons of two tall and skinny buildings. Dark metal and piles of dirt and materials around it. A big curtain covered one side of most of the bottom. I wondered out loud what was being built but no one seemed to understand what I said in Spanish.

The Monday after we visited the Statue of Liberty, Mami took us to the school down the block. I remember that we spent many hours completing the admissions process. A chubby and sweet lady, as I had never seen before, gave us a tour of the school. We walked behind her as we listened attentively to her half-broken Spanish when she explained the various sections of the school. This was the biggest school I had ever visited and the ugliest as well. The walls were pale blue, and the ceilings were high. The windows were tall and covered with dirt and iron gates. They looked like they had never been cleaned before as they were full of dust. They had streaks of dry goo dripping down the glass panels. The only clean part of the school was the floor and the little light that reflected from a few of the windows made it shine like a mirror. The entire school had a particular smell that tickled my nose. I sneezed several times throughout the visit, and my eyes were teary many times.

Mami signed papers, and we took some assessments on papers. I did not know how to complete parts of my test since it was all in English and had patterns of little dots. Months later, I learned that those patterns were meant to select multiple-choice answers to questions. Math was the easy part, and I took pride in knowing that my answers were correct. Ody was given a different test with only pictures, and Angel and Loli just stared at me as if to want my help. They, too, must not have understood the English parts of the test. At some point, a lady came and asked for the papers with a motion. She collected the tests and the pencils she had given us a few minutes earlier. She looked through them and made an expression that wrinkled all her forehead, then smiled at some point. The translator came in a while later and told Mami that we had done very well in math but obviously did not complete the English part. We sat quietly the rest of the time, waiting for Mami to complete all the paperwork. Mami had promised to take us for ice cream once we were done with registration at school.

After leaving school that day, a feeling of sadness invaded my soul. Instead of moving to middle school as I was supposed to, Mami had agreed to place me in fifth grade again to facilitate my English learning. The principal said, via the translator, that soon they would be opening elementary bilingual programs in the city and I would do much better there than in the middle school in the neighborhood where there were gangs and fighting all the time. After explaining that to us, the principal turned to me and gave me a look over her glasses and patted my shoulder as she gave me a half smile.

I silently cried all that night and many of the nights after that. Since I was the oldest child, I was not allowed to cry unless something really hurt physically. Mami would hit us if she found anyone crying without a cause. She was usually very busy and had no time for made-up stuff and complaints, she always said. Early on, she told us how the laws in New York forbade parents from hitting their children, but she could care less about those laws and would get to us if we ever reported her to the authorities. Her favorite punishment was a smack on the head with her knuckles, which left you dizzy for a moment and created a bump that was sore for days. She was very fast at it, and there was never time to react and run away from it. Only Loli had mastered the art of escaping those, but eventually Mami would catch up to her with a double whammy when my sister was just sitting around and had forgotten about the misbehavior.

The Saturday before school began, Mami took us shopping for our school supplies, and we spent the day at the stores. We returned home with lots of bags filled with clothes and school supplies that were on the list she got when we went to school for registration. I remember feeling very nervous on the days before school started. The night before, I sat in bed all night, waiting for daylight to symbolize a new day. Once I saw the first daylight, I hopped out of bed to be the first one to use the bathroom. There were six of us sharing the same bathroom, and mornings were always hectic at our home. I was always the first one in, and I mastered the skill of doing things very fast. Since the day we went to admissions at school, every day I wondered what school in New York would be like and how my classmates would treat me since I did not speak their language. I had already experienced feelings of loneliness while visiting the park every Saturday. I was not able to understand anything anyone said around me. The few times I heard people speak Spanish, it made me very happy, and I felt comforted that there were other people like us. Somehow my little sister, Ody, had learned some English during the summer and was able to communicate with people at the park, but she was young and not yet able to read.

The summer of '71 was very interesting for all of us. A lot of things happened for the first time. We traveled by plane, rode the subway, lived in an apartment building, and went swimming at a public pool that was crowded with people we did not know. We went up an elevator to a very tall building, and although that gave me butterflies in my stomach and clogged my ears, I discovered that I liked heights. We visited the biggest store in the world, which smelled like a giant perfume box, and saw mannequins wearing various interesting and colorful outfits and big wigs. We also climbed the Statue of Liberty by those narrow spiral steps. We learned our first words in English, which Papi taught us during dinner time. Although Mami said we were just here for a few years, I sensed deep inside me that we were here to stay and that New York had become our permanent home.

MIDNIGHT MOVE

Moving to East 163rd Street near the Grand Concourse was one of the main family events for the summer of '71. Since our arrival, Daddy said that the original living arrangements were only temporary.

"We will work hard to provide a safe place for you," he said to us soon after our arrival to New York.

The building we lived in on Morris Avenue was not a safe place to raise children; I heard my parents whisper to each other several times. There was urine on the stairwells at times. There were many people whose smoke clouded the hallways all day, and that smoke seeped through the crack under the door. Loud music of all kinds emerged from people's apartments. Other families quarreled all the time, and we could hear their loud voices in what I assumed were not nice words for each other. Later, I learned that my parents' apartment had been robbed weeks prior to our arrival, and the thieves took most things of value, including my parents' wedding box with heirloom items and the family photo albums. They never told us that story because they did not want to scare us. Over the years, my parents have collected some of our baby pictures from family members back in the homeland. Mami said that she cried for many days after the burglary because after that she did not have pictures of her children while they were separated.

The last Friday in August, Mami came home early from work with several empty boxes and announced that on that evening we would be moving to a larger apartment in the building where the elderly cousins lived. Since we did not own much, we packed very quickly, and by the time Papi came home, all our stuff had been placed in boxes and the clothes folded in the few suitcases and bags we owned. Mami asked me to pack the kitchen stuff and gave me two boxes, where I carefully placed all the glass and chinaware. I used newspaper, towels, and linen to protect the fragile items. Remembering how Mami packed for our last move a few years before helped me to do a nice job packing for that brisk move.

Papi arrived with a few cousins, each with a supermarket shopping cart where they packed as many boxes as possible. "Vámonos," he said as they rolled the stuff down the three and half blocks to 163 Street to the new place. Once at the new building, other cousins and the building superintendent helped carry the boxes and furniture up the four flights of stairs. During one of the many trips carrying our belongings in small carts, one of the helping cousins clumsily turned the television cart, which was carrying mattresses and dropped the stuff in the middle of the street. The cars passing by had to maneuver around to proceed while my dad and the guys helping picked up the mattresses and proceeded ahead with the moving. Later, when we told Mami what had occurred, she was quite perturbed by the idea that our mattresses could very well acquire so many germs while on the ground. She was also concerned as to who had witnessed the chaos. "Ay, Dios mio!" she exclaimed while listening to the story. So before we went to bed, I had to help Mami disinfect the mattresses with a bleach solution she had prepared in a bucket. Only then were we allowed to make the beds and go to sleep on those mattresses.

The kids helped as much as possible, and by midnight, we were moved in, and the beds had been assembled for us to sleep that night. I do not remember if my parents were able to assemble their big bed or if they were able to get any rest that night. When I woke up the next morning with the smell of coffee and burned cinnamon,

I found Mami almost done with arranging the kitchen stuff into the cabinets and the refrigerator. She asked me to help her with the younger kids to ensure they bathed and were settled in their spaces in our bedroom. That Saturday, Papi was free from work, and he announced that he also was free that Monday. Since we arrived, my dad had worked every day except Sundays, and we were only able to be around him a few hours during dinner and before bedtime every day. Every time he was near us, he showered us with hugs and kisses and made us laugh incessantly.

At the new apartment, the eat-in kitchen was ample, and in it, there was a big refrigerator as well as a pantry and a separate utility closet. There was a big walk-in closet in the living room and a smaller closet in the hallway. Each bedroom had a closet as well. This was a big improvement from our first apartment, which only had two small closets. There was no wallpaper anywhere in the new apartment, and my parents had it painted a beautiful cream color.

They bought new living room furniture a few weeks later and acquired other used furniture from a neighbor who was moving away to a place called Ohio. The entrance to this apartment had a long narrow hallway, and there were three sets of panels on the wall which matched the crown molding on top of the walls that met the high white ceiling. All the rooms had crown molding and matching base-boards which were elaborate and neat. Those were all painted white. I noticed that the window borders also matched the design on all the boards. I imagined that someday if I were allowed to design a home, I would like to have similar details in it.

Moving a few blocks away from our arrival home made a differ-ence in lifestyle. We moved to an apartment in the same building as our elderly cousins. I heard Mami say that it would facilitate child-care issues until my abuela Abi was able to come from the Dominican Republic and help with caring for us while my parents worked. The new apartment was almost twice the size as the original one. Again, my parents arranged for us to take the master bedroom because it was much bigger. That bedroom was big, with a large closet and two tall windows. There was a fire escape on one of the windows. In this bed-room, my parents arranged four twin beds, two dressers with three drawers for each one of us, a wardrobe stand, and a desk. There was still room to walk around and play.

Initially, there were no loud sirens in the middle of the night at the new apartment. There were no loud neighbors quarreling in the middle of the night or early in the morning. The alley that connected the three buildings that met toward the back was clean and clear of debris. It seemed that every apartment had a clothesline to hang wet clothes. Ours hung from the kitchen window and attached from a hook that lined up toward the middle of the building next door. Floor by floor, all the clotheslines were lined from a metal hook. Mami did not allow us kids to hang anything from the clothesline since she said we might fall out the window and end in the alley- way splashed all over the hard pavement. Many times, when I heard Mami caution us about safety, I thought she exaggerated much. She worried all the time about us and constantly prayed for our safety.

There were many "not to do" rules added to the existing list when we moved to the new apartment. Because some of the windows were wide and low, there were safety bars on each one of them. We were not allowed to even touch the safety bars in case we pushed too hard and fell out the windows. We were to continue to remain indoors unless either of our parents went out with us, and finally, we were not allowed to watch television past nine in the evening once school began.

The move to the new apartment was drastic and impromptus, but it improved how I viewed our transition to the new country. Cramped in the first apartment had incited me to question my parents' decision to come to the United States. I often inquired about their motives to move to North America. When they dismissed my questioning, I remained pensive about the topic. "Why did we come here?" I often asked.

The new apartment gave me many fond memories and set some of the foundation for many of my decisions for years to come. We lived at that place for five years, and those were enough to determine where home was and to set goals for what I would aspire to do and want when I became an adult. It was at the apartment on 163rd Street that I learned many life skills and experienced many firsts here in the new country. Whenever I dreamed of home, it was the images of that home where the setting took place. Even in the nightmares about army tanks following me, it was to that home that I ran to for refuge, in my dreams.

I spent many hours staring out the window next to my bed and watching how people behaved and interacted in the streets. Out there, on Sherman Avenue, there were people of all types, shapes, ages, gender, colors, social class. They interacted with each other and went about daily routines. Some seemed to ignore each other even when they walked at the same pace and direction. Others assisted each other when in need, like when a woman ran after an elderly lady who was getting wet in the rain and offered her umbrella for protection. There was another time when a kid ran in front of a car and a young man passing by pulled him back just in time before he was run over. A few just occupied space, either sitting at the stoops in front of buildings or leaning on someone else's car for hours on end. I assume that most people I watched were rushing about catching up with busy life in this city, just like my parents.

There was little need for me to want to go outside, and Mami's imposition of remaining indoors all the time seemed to bother me less than what troubled my siblings. I enjoyed snow days when we were forced to remain indoors and was grateful that I did not have to shovel the snow like some of the kids I saw out the window. I was also thankful that I did not have to fend for myself out there as I saw other kids do because some did not have a safe homelife to turn to when they needed support. My new life in this new country and the desire to thrive and succeed began to take shape in the summer of '71, and I have carried that yearning to always move ahead for the next fifty years of my life.

WHILE AT EAST 163 STREET

In search of a more comfortable and safer environment, our family moved overnight to East 163 Street; it was a six-story building walk-up three and a half blocks from where we had originally arrived over a month earlier. The new apartment was in a larger, cleaner building with brightly lit hallways. The stairs were wide, and it was much easier to step up to the fourth floor, where we lived. Our apartment was spacious enough that we did not have to feel like we lived on top of each other. The main door had three locks, of which one was called a police lock with a long iron stick which prevented the door from opening if the stick was in lock position. The door was heavy and made a loud bang if one let it go upon entering. We were all careful not to let it swing since it was one of Mami's rules: "no slamming doors." That apartment had very tall windows, and sunlight came in abundance at an angle in the kids' bedroom every afternoon.

The Saturday morning after the move, Mami took me across the street with her to help do the laundry. The laundromat was directly across the street from our new building, and right next to it, there was a grocery store where we shopped for last-minute items like milk and eggs. Sometimes Daddy used to help the store owner, and eventually he became the store manager when that owner retired to Puerto Rico.

Mami taught me how to use the machines in the laundromat, and I was curious to learn this new skill. "Watch how I do these things," she said. There were rows of big washing machines toward the entrance and a section for dryers in the back with big folding tables in the middle of the large room. It cost a quarter to wash a load and a dime for ten minutes of drying time. A large boom box radio on top of the change machine always played the Z100 station to popular songs. The laundromat smelled fresh, and sometimes the smell of fabric softener was dragged down the street by the wind.

I had never seen a washing machine before nor been in a place where many machines did all the wash instead of people. Back in the old country, a lady came along once a week and spent the day hand-washing all our clothes. At Abuelo's farm, on the wash days, some of the older cousins often washed the clothes by hand in big pails close to the ground.

In the old country, Mami would also iron all the bed sheets and Daddy's underwear. I often wondered if that was necessary. In New York, maintaining clothes seemed to have become easier, and that made me happy because now I was Mami's laundry helper.

Mami folded the clothes as soon as they came out of the dryer. "There would be no need to iron most of them," she said. The big folding tables were up to my chest at first, but with time, they seemed to get shorter for me. She taught me how to fold each item of clothing in very precise ways to avoid ironing. The clothes were very hot out of the dryer, and at times I burned my skinny arms with zippers or buttons. "If you allow the clothes to get wrinkled, you will be responsible for ironing them," Mami said in a sharp tone. So I learned quickly how to fold them properly.

Bobbing my head side to side, I folded the clothes very fast. The sound of disco music emanated from the boom box above. The background music helped me forget the heat emerging from the hot clothing items and avoid the chatter that women created about their life issues. With time, I learned the words to "Rock the Boat," "Just

My Imagination," "Imagine," "Got to Be There," and many other songs.

There were always five loads of laundry every week, and Mami showed me how to color coordinate each load. The towels were all washed together, and the sheets were also a separate load. There were six of us at home before my grandmother Abi joined us the following spring after we arrived.

At home, when we prepared the laundry, Mami would separate each pile on the floor, and I would quickly stuff each pile into pillowcases. Then we would carry those piles in the shopping cart to the laundromat.

Rolling the cart down the corner through a very narrow path with mounds of snow on both sides became a challenge each time. Sometimes the cart would get stuck in the snow mud, and Mami and I had to push very hard to get the little wheels moving again. Although Mami was a small-framed lady with a bony body, she was strong, and at times, I had seen her push very big and heavy things out of the way.

One day, when the snow came down very high while we were at the laundromat, on the way home Mami picked up the whole cart and carried it over the big piles of snow so that the clean clothes would not get dirty. That time I gave a side-eye look at the two young men who watched and cheered her on and said how beautiful she was instead of helping her. I walked beside her carrying one bag with the detergent and another with the wet clothes to be air-dried at home. After crossing the street, I looked back at those young men and stuck my tongue out at them, hoping Mami would not see me doing that. I made sure Mami wasn't looking when I did mischievous things to adults because I did not want to get punished afterward. I wanted to avoid her wrath.

My family lived peacefully on East 163rd Street, and our neighbors were mostly nice to one another. Most adults in our building worked during the day, and all the children attended school. Several older ladies with gray hair remained home and visited the nearby park in the afternoons. My siblings and I often saw the older ladies returning from the park when we were coming back from school.

Some of them often looked at us with disdain and made comments which I did not understand at first. The building was very silent during the night. During the day on weekends, the soft sounds of various music types emerged from various apartments as we climbed the four flights to our apartment after returning from the supermarket with the groceries. The teen girls who lived next to the elderly cousins played disco music all the time until their parents came home. An elderly lady on the third floor played classical music on the piano in the afternoons. When at home, Daddy played Spanish ballads on the record player. With time, many of the older ladies moved away. Later, I heard many of them moved to a new building complex called Co-op City.

A few summers after we moved to 163rd Street, a new family moved in and changed the mood of our building. That family lived two stories below our apartment, but we could hear their loud music at all hours of the day and sometimes at night. They also quarreled many times, and their screams at each other could be heard throughout the building. They had the habit of leaving their door open while they cooked, and the smell of fried food would permeate throughout the entire building as well. Soon after they moved in, their friends who visited also became a nuisance since they used to sit in the stairwell by their apartment and smoke all types of smelly things. From the conversations the adults were having, I discovered that the strong smell of burning herbs that often came through the bedroom window in the middle of the night was called marijuana. The cousins down on the first floor had been talking about and discussing the new neighbors' behavior and mentioned their smoking habits with disdain and disgust. The elderly cousin told my siblings and I how that herb could fry a person's brain and make them useless.

"That is a bad habit," he said to us repeatedly. From that day on, I was careful to cover my nose and hold my breath as I walked upstairs and passed by the new neighbors' door. I did not want to become useless, I thought to myself.

On a particular Sunday, as we returned home from one of our city outings with Mami, we stumbled upon two young men sitting lamely outside the door to the new neighbors' apartment.

"Excuse me," said Mami several times. Since they did not move when we asked, we had to hop around them to go up the steps. As we got to the stairs landing above, I looked back and recognized one of them as the guy who had whistled at Mami while she carried our laundry cart over a pile of snow months before. Again, I gave him a side-eye and on my way up, thought that the elderly cousins were right, that smelly herb could fry your brain.

As soon as we walked into our apartment, Mami summoned my siblings and I to the dining table and gave us a lecture about what we had just seen out by the stairwell on our way up. She became agitated when she talked to us about some of the dangers encountered in the city where we lived. She made us each promise that we would never, ever, ever do anything that would turn us into people like the ones we had just seen downstairs. "Nunca, nunca," she repeated several times. After the speech, Mami prayed over us and blessed each one so that God may always protect and keep us from any evil.

Half a century later, Mami continues to be a devout Catholic, and prayer is always her way out of any peril. She and Daddy read the Bible every day and prayed the rosary at night. A picture of "El Corazon de Jesus," Jesus and the Cross, always adorned the entrance of our home, as well as a small statue of the Virgin Mary was part of every bedroom. Mami belonged to the ladies' prayer group at church, and by the time I turned thirteen, she enrolled my sister Loli and me into the youth group Daughters of Mary after we received our Confirmation rite.

That evening after the stairwell incident, Daddy also lectured us during dinnertime. He was more technical about explaining to us the impact of drugs on families. Although Daddy was mostly less dramatic than Mami, that time he told us stories of people he had known at work who had lost everything, including their families, due to addictions. He graphically explained to us how dealers would trick kids to carry out messages and merchandise for them, and eventually kids would end up in a very bad place and ruin their lives. "Mucho cuidado, niños," Daddy cautioned us with much passion.

That night, after Mami tucked us in bed and shut off the lights, my siblings and I wondered in a whisper how the people we saw laying down by the stairs smoking habits had ruined their lives and come to upset our peaceful building. We also wondered how much of what our parents had told us that weekend was much exaggeration or fear.

"They are scared," said Loli about our parents.

When my siblings had already fallen asleep and I remained awake thinking, I promised myself that I would never end up like those guys in the stairwell or like some others I had seen looking like zombies along the streets on our way to school. At that point, I had no idea what those zombie-like people were, but they sure did not look healthy nor useful. My abuelo's words resonated in my head when I had these thoughts. Before we left our old country, Abuelo said to always make our family name proud. "Con mucho orgullo," he'd said then.

Years later, after graduating college with a psychology degree, I worked as a drug education counselor. I felt out of place in that job since I was one of the few workers who was a "square." I did that job for less than a year before moving on to graduate school to become a regular educator. During my career, I tried to guide teenagers into selecting the most productive path. I taught them about the coping skills that helped me overcome the challenges I faced growing up in a hostile and demanding environment. "You must have goals, or someone will decide for you what your path will be," I always told my students.

AT THE CAFETERIA

It was a windy day in September. My hair was blown into my face, and a curl went into my mouth as I talked to my sister. It was my first day of school in New York City. For me, that day was crammed with many first events and experiences. School began in the middle of the week after Labor Day. My siblings and I were excited about getting to wear the new clothes Mami bought for us the weekend before.

Upon arriving at school that morning, all students had to wait inside the tall black iron fence until teachers called our names. We were all lined up by the teacher who had called us. Parents remained on the sidewalk and watched as lines of kids entered the school building before leaving.

Mami waved when I looked her way. I was very nervous and did not understand any of the instructions, so I decided to follow what everyone else was doing, hoping that I would not end up in the wrong place. My siblings went away with other groups in different directions.

Although I think I have a simple first and last name, since arriving in the new country, oftentimes people mispronounced either or both names. I had to listen carefully the second time a lady called my name because she pronounced it funny to my ears. When she called my name again, I raised my hand as other students ahead of me had done.

After she finished roll call, she signaled me to follow her and then called another little girl. She spoke in English to the little girl who then turned to me and translated to Spanish what this teacher had said. I understood that this little girl who I just met would become my school partner for the next few weeks so that I could understand what was going on. My new classmate, Eli, became my translator and guide at that school. I immediately admired that she could communicate in two languages.

That first day of school, Eli wore a blue dress like me and had two long ponytails like mine. My new teacher led our group around the back of the building and up three flights of stairs. Our classroom felt damp, and it had a smell of metal and markers. There were posters hanging on all the walls. The lights were bright, and sunrays seemed to shine against the large but dull windows. The teacher smiled, and I assumed she welcomed the class.

I recall that this school was very different from my old school. I had studied at a boarding school with nuns since my parents left for New York. Before that, I attended the same nun's school but did not live there. Unlike that place, this school was large, and no one wore uniforms. The teachers did not wear a habit, nor was there any prayer time before class began. There was no raising of the flag nor singing of the national anthem that morning. At some point in time, we all stood up in class, and some kids placed their right hand over their chest as modeled by the teacher. A voice came over the loudspeaker, and some kids in class recited something like what was said over the airway. Days later, I learned that it was the Pledge of Allegiance; learning its words would take me about a year, and feeling its message took about another decade.

After a few class lessons and activities which I did not understand, we headed to the cafeteria. It was a large room void of natural lighting. The little windows high above on the walls were dirty and covered with some metal grid, which did not allow much sunlight to enter except for a small corner at the back of the large room, where a rectangle of light reflected on a long table. There were long tables with seats attached, shaped like the ones at the picnic section of the park. The floor was shiny but painted in a dark dull brown color. Thick square columns everywhere interfered with the flow of the room, and the ceiling was not as high as the one in the classroom.

I followed Eli everywhere she went. She showed me the line for getting our lunch when a teacher instructed the kids at our table to get up. I picked up a tray, on which I placed a little plastic bag with a napkin and utensils. I asked Eli about the little red and brown boxes, and she explained that it was milk and that I would probably like the brown one. The brown box was wet and cold to the touch. I continued to mimic her actions and grabbed a small square plate with something that looked like wet cat food on it. Getting the plate closer to me, I realized what that awful smell was when we first entered the cafeteria, and it made me gag.

Eli waited for me to finish placing the food items on my tray, and we walked together to a table where we placed our trays and sat down to eat. "Come todo," she said to me as she began to eat all her food. I stared at the items on my tray and wondered what to do with some of them. There was a small plastic bag, and when I took out the items in it, I did not recognize what one of the things was. I assumed that someone had made a mistake when creating something that looked like a spoon, but it had three spikes at the end. I took out the little napkin and placed it on my lap. I also made sure to keep my elbows off the table. At some point, I realized a few girls sitting at the other side of the long table, but across from me, were pointing and laughing at me. I gave them my usual side-eye and was bothered by their mockery of whatever it was they had noticed about me. Later, when I asked Eli why those girls had laughed at me, she said that I was too proper for this school. "Eres muy fina," she said as she laughed.

After lunch, our group returned to our homeroom, where our teacher was waiting with a math lesson on the board. Although I did not understand any of her instructions nor her explanations, I was able to complete all the work easily. I had done this type of math two years ago, and multiplication and division had been my strengths since I had memorized the timetable when I was in third grade. I had become a math tutor at my old school when I was in the sixth grade. Now I was beginning fifth grade again, and I could already sense I was going to need a lot of patience, but admitted that I also had a long way to go while I learned the new language.

When we were dismissed from school that first day of school, Mrs. Rosa, the elderly cousin, was waiting for my siblings and me outside the school gate. I was very happy to see a familiar face and that the first day of school had finally ended. Mrs. Rosa took us to her home, where we waited for Mami to return from work. At Mrs. Rosa's home, we mostly sat quietly in the living room. She offered us the snacks that Mami had given her that morning. As we sat patiently waiting for Mami's return, Mrs. Rosa went about with house chores and cooking for her family.

"Mami, Mami." We made a big fuss when she came to pick us up after work that day. We all had lots of stories to share with her about our first day of school, and she desperately tried to listen to all four of us talking at once. Mami gave me the keys to our apartment so that I could rush ahead and open the door. My siblings followed her to our fourth-floor apartment while tugging at her arms and chatting all at once. Each one wanted her undivided attention that day. I was very happy to be home after what seemed to be a very long chain of events at school.

That evening, at the dinner table, we took turns to tell our stories to both Mami and Papi. They listened attentively and encouraged details and explanations while controlling our impulses to all talk at once. Papi made connections to other stories from the past and his own childhood. Mami remained at the table longer than usual so she could listen again to all the details about our exciting day. She wanted to hear about the food at school and the bathroom facilities and if the teachers were nice to us. We all talked and laughed. Talked some more and laughed again. That evening, we talked longer than ever, and when we were done with dinner, it was already time to get ready for bed.

Every night before going to bed, it was my job to ensure that my younger siblings had brushed their teeth and washed up. They were also to prepare and set aside their clothes for the next day and leave it all on a hanger by the front of the closet. Everyone's bookbag was also to be left in the living room ready for the next morning. Mami would come in to inspect everything, bless each one of us, and pray before turning the lights off. That night, I was very tired and fell asleep as soon as Mami shut the lights off. It had been a very eventful and challenging day filled with many first experiences. I was elated to be home and safe.

REFLECTIONS OF A CHILD

The room was spinning every night I lay on my bed during the first week of school. I felt as if my bed was being rocked from side to side, and my body still felt tense from the events that happened every school day. I felt palpitations as I thought about the kids throwing food in the cafeteria, the fights in the playground, and my lack of understanding my teacher while she explained every lesson other than math.

My bed was at the extreme corner of the room, and the metal headboard leaned against one of the two windows in the room. My mattress was firm, and I often lay on my back until I fell asleep. Many thoughts and images crossed my mind every night. I remember feeling very tired, although I had not done much physical activity any of those days.

Over the years, I continued to remember those first days of school in New York as if they were rewound movie scenes, frame by frame. I remember nervously shaking most of the time in school. My hands were often sweaty, although the temperature was cool. The image of the girls laughing and mocking me the first day of school came to my memory, and that made me very sad. I was also upset because the food in the cafeteria made me gag. I didn't even have to taste the thing that looked like wet cat food to know that it tasted awful. I had never liked eating anything that had lumps, nor that was too wet. At home, I often got reprimanded when soup or stew was served as a meal. During the night thoughts, I also remembered that when I tasted the chocolate milk, I almost gagged because the chocolate didn't even taste like cocoa. The only thing that I ate for lunch those days was the bun that although cold, was the only familiar taste. When Mami asked how the food was, I did not share with her that I did not eat because I did not want to get reprimanded.

My heart was pounding hard the whole first day of school and for many days after that. Although it was very noisy, I could hear the echo of my heartbeat after there was a fight in the cafeteria the first day. Some kids on the other side of the cafeteria threw food up in the air and splashed milk on several kids sitting at my table. My new friend and I were spared getting splashed with food or milk. I had never seen kids fight in front of adults who were there to watch them. The cafeteria experience made me realize that my life in our new city was that of new beginnings. Whenever thoughts of the school approached my head, they made me wonder how I would be able to navigate being a new student in the Bronx. I was cognizant that I had to work very hard just to live my new life since school was such an integral part of my life. So school life made me very pensive.

I remember being a precocious child from the time I had memory of things, and always inquisitive about life and my surroundings. Silently watching people and learning from them brought me joy. Sometimes I learned what not to do from watching the mistakes of others. Mental lists of what I would not do and what I would emulate were common practices. I observed without judging unless it was about me. Whenever I visited the countryside of the Dominican Republic, I was fascinated by the body language and the expressions people made while speaking to each other. People used their bodies to indicate many things such as pointing the location of an object. My abuela Abi often pointed with her lips to indicate the direction of an object or threw her arms up in the air and held her head when I read bad news in the newspaper. I enjoyed watching Maria, the lady who helped Mami with household chores when we lived in Boca Chica. Maria was always humming to a tune, and I found rhythm in her moves while she washed the laundry and hung them in the backyard clothes lines.

While visiting my abuelo's farm, the ladies who ground the coffee in big mortars were also fascinating. Two ladies would each use a big pestle to hit in the mortar in synchronized harmony to finely grind the coffee beans after roasting them in a big pan close to the ground. While doing this task, these ladies would often listen to stories on the radio which narrated dramatic events that had to do with crime. As they worked, they argued and laughed about the events being narrated on the radio and made connections to stories happening around town. Meanwhile, I glanced at them and listened to the sound of the mortar from up above the jabillo tree while I read one of the books left behind by Papi.

Somehow, adults talked about grown-up conversations in my presence. At times they whispered, but I could still hear what they said. Perhaps they assumed that I was in my own world of childhood. I was often reading a book or engaged in some craft project. I enjoyed crocheting, drawing, and sewing clothes for my dolls. But as they talked about life events, I listened and absorbed all types of information pertaining to human relationships, running a household, raising children in the sixties and seventies, family finances, political ideologies, social strife and religion, and just plain common-sense issues which were my abuela Abi's favorite topics. By the age of nine, I had assumed a rather acute precocity which some saw as obnoxious, while others deemed charming.

The term *bookworm* applied to me very well. Sometimes people teased me about it, and frankly, I never minded being called that by neither kids nor adults. I enjoyed immersing myself into reading and writing. I read everything available from fiction, philosophy books, the classics, poetry, essays, and news editor corner. If it had printed words, I would be reading its content.

I remember themes of love, death and living, free will, and human existence. I recall how engrossed I became in every story's plot and characters. *El Lazarillo de Tormes* was one of my favorite stories. It related the life of a boy whose mother had to give him away because she was not able to care for him. Some of the stories I read made me think about my own existence and circumstances. During my early teen years, I read Walt Whitman and the poems "Song of Myself" and "Leaves of Grass." Those writings captivated my interest and made me ponder about my own mortality and existence. I was able to understand their full meaning only later in life.

I was already in high school when I discovered the main public library in midtown Manhattan. Walking in for the first time made me feel like I had gone to heaven. Many hours immersed in piles of books was a common occurrence for me. Walking through the tall stacks of fiction and philosophy books made me feel safe and at home. Sometimes, I sat right on the floor, where I found an interesting book. Imagining that the author spoke to me directly made me feel comfortable. All distractions disappeared for me when I just read for hours. I often found myself leaning against a shelf for a long time and read there amid knowledge. My friend Jackie preferred to sit on a chair by the windows and knew where to find me when it was time to go home.

Occasionally, I borrowed a library book or two and read it at home in a few days. Reading became an excuse to ask my parents for permission to visit the library the following week. "Otro libro!" Mami would say in amazement whenever I requested permission to go to the library in midtown. If she ever asked for the content of a book, I was always glad to give her a synopsis of the plot, and she often reminded me not to take book plots too personally.

There were few people who I could talk to about my active reading while growing up. Oftentimes my older cousin's husband, Yamil, was one of those people who would engage into substantial conversations and would discuss and explain to me the meanings of some readings. He would encourage more reading and making connections between one reading and another. Yamil and his wife lived near us only for a while.

Later, Father O'Hara became my spiritual mentor. He was the old parish priest who was very well liked by every youth at church. Father O'Hara walked the neighborhood carrying a shillelagh, and I watched him use it as a tool for all necessities, including defending himself around the neighborhood's tough streets. He pointed out to me that many books were written by authors who were influenced by stories from the Bible. Oftentimes, we compared fiction characters with those from the Holy Book. He also explained to me how songs were poems, and many poems were stories mostly told by men whose heart had been broken. Other songs narrated the struggles of a people. He introduced me to the writings of Edgar Allan Poe and Steinbeck. We discussed "The Raven," and once after community service, we walked to Poe's old house on the Grand Concourse.

"Poetry is a beautiful way to discover many of life's issues and social ills," Father O'Hara said. When salsa music became popular in the seventies, many songs told the stories of lost love and social issues. Many weekends during the summertime, the songs emanating from people's homes contained lyrics that were very poetic and addressed the issues that Father O'Hara explained.

Since the windows to everyone's apartments were open during the summer, the music emerged at a distance. The summer when the song "*periódico de ayer...*" or "Yesterday's newspaper..." became popular, one could hear various households play that song throughout the day and night. It told the story of a man who's loved one left him. Like this Spanish song, songs from the movie *Saturday Night Fever* played all day and night. Father O'Hara and I talked about these songs whenever we had a chance. I volunteered at the church rectory or at the elderly care facility in the neighborhood where he supervised the youth ministry.

I used to write about my thoughts since I was very young. I wrote about the event I experienced during my first week of school in New York City public schools. I think that I learned to make lists of things to do around that time in my life. It was not until I reached ninth grade that I learned that practice was called journaling. My English teacher introduced journaling as a tool to release disturbing thoughts about everyday life. She would say that journaling would help with the pains of growing up. In my journal, I wrote about likes and dislikes. I wrote about plans and goals. I remember making lists of things I will never do or be. As time went on, I continued to write about perturbing events and issues. Journaling became my place of solace for all those ideas that kept me awake at night. Journaling made me feel less alone in a city full of strangers and a household full of people.

THE BIG TV

Few and simple items adorned our home when we first arrived in this country. Slowly my parents began to acquire things to fill in the empty spaces in our apartment. When our neighbors next door moved away during the fall of '71, Mami bought several of their furniture pieces to continue to furnish our bigger apartment. Among those was a big TV set, one with a built-in cabinet and small speakers on the side. It also had a little box with an antenna which we did not have to jiggle around like the old TV. The kids were so happy about this new acquisition that we talked about it as if it were another family member. Especially happy was my brother, Angel, who was truly convinced that it was the biggest and most important thing in our home. Many times, he tried to monopolize its use and wanted to watch his favorite cartoons. He loved Superman and Spiderman and mimicked their actions to nauseum.

The images on TV at the time had strange coloring. The colors on TV were never true to the ones in actual life. It seemed as if the scenes had been painted over with pale ink. In the early seventies, there were only about eight channels. Mami said we were lucky that there was a Spanish channel by the time we arrived here. When she and Papi got here a couple of years before, "the Spanish channel was just being inaugurated and showing was limited," they said. At the time, they only had a small black-and-white TV, which did not have good reception. Although we kids preferred the shows on English channels, we had to watch the Spanish news and talk shows when Papi wanted to watch TV.

My favorite show was *Casper the Friendly Ghost*. It was relaxing to watch him float around the place. I remember that we were not able to pronounce the word *ghost* and made attempts to sound it out as best we could. One day, one of the adult cousins taught us how to pronounce the word after making mockery of us. English was very complicated at the time. Of the kids, Ody was the only one able to speak a little English then, but she was not able to read complicated words since she was only in first grade.

I often wondered why syllables were not pronounced the same every time and why the vowels had different sounds. It was very confusing to pronounce this new language, and it made me nervous every time I had to read out loud in school or had to explain a question in class. Although I was able to understand most of what I read, pronouncing and writing dictation words in English class was a big challenge for a while. At school, I enjoyed the phonics class with all the color charts and workbooks that showed how syllables were pronounced. I would memorize the color chart and the pronunciations so I would not make mistakes when I read in class. At the end of phonics class, my cheeks always hurt from moving my mouth in so many new ways. The teacher also came up with the idea that students went over some words out loud at home before going to bed at night. It took some months for my mouth to get used to the new and various mouth positions for pronunciation. After learning how to pronounce the word *ghost*, I wondered how many other words were written in such strange way.

With the new TV, a new set of rules was implemented at home. TV viewing was limited to afternoons and then after dinner until 9:00 p.m. if we had completed our homework. The rules were strict. Once, Daddy caught my siblings and I watching TV past curfew time when he arrived late from selling home products. We were so focused on the show that we did not notice he arrived and was just staring at us from the end of the hallway. After reprimanding us with his look, he blessed each one and sent us all to bed immediately. Daddy knew each time we stayed late to watch TV, and at his first chance, during dinner, he would bring up the importance of following rules and engaging in other activities instead of TV. He was convinced that TV had bad influence on children and that even cartoons showed much violence and other misbehaviors. He was totally opposed to us watching telenovelas or any shows that displayed much of popular culture with dysfunctional issues. We sat through many of his lectures about maintaining a simple lifestyle and working hard and learning constructive things so that we could someday become respectful professionals.

It was still warm outside when the last street party was celebrated. Mami would not allow us to join any of the street parties during the summer. We did not participate in any street festivities. Not even on the day there was a portable pool that was pulled by a big truck were we allowed to go downstairs. She claimed those gatherings were dangerous and would not contribute to anything good for us. So we were left to watch the street parties from our bedroom windows up on the fourth floor. Other kids were allowed to join the festivities, and yet others were allowed to climb out the fire escape window and watch from outside their windows. We were not even allowed to stick our heads out the windows even though there were safety gates on each window.

One day, Angel decided to play the Penguin from *Batman* and climbed out the fire escape when Mami was busy in the kitchen. He may have jumped trying to imitate that character if it had not been for Ody calling us to have ice cream which Mami prepared for us. My responsibility was to watch my siblings when Mami was busy in the kitchen. That day, just as I noticed Angel's intentions, I was glad for Ody's timing. I assumed then that Daddy was correct by saying that too much TV could harm kids. Years later, Angel would join the US Army Special Forces and become a sergeant with the Eighty-Second Airborne. He jumped from planes, and I guess, he got to become his own version of the Penguin then.

That night at dinnertime, Angel inquired about what would happen if he played Batman out on the fire escape, and it was then when Mami implemented additional set of rules of safety to the ones already in place. Our apartment had become our cage, where inside was the only safe place on earth according to our mother. Daddy always agreed with whatever Mami said about discipline since she was the one to implement the rules and beat us with *the chancleta* if we did not follow them. Although I often followed the rules, I got hit several times because I was the one in charge of making sure my younger siblings behaved. Eventually I spoke to Mami about her practice of punishing me for the behaviors of others, and I was happy when she stopped hitting me altogether.

TV became one of the windows to the outside world for my siblings and me. Since we were seldom allowed outside our home other than school and church, that form of entertainment was the easiest for us to see how life was outside our immediate family and our four walls at home. School was also interesting, and eventually Mami allowed us to participate in all school trips and musical events. Mami also continued to take us to the park most Saturdays when it was good weather, and our tours of the city were always welcomed activities by all.

Most times I watched TV, I also did something else. I enjoyed working on several hobbies. So one could say I listened to TV most times. While my siblings quarreled over which show to watch, I was happy to just enjoy other creative things to do. I read every day and read even more when I could finally do so in two languages. When not at school, I spent most of the time at home either reading or working on some creative project. I also learned how to play the recorder and hoped to someday move on to other instruments if possible. I joined the school choir, and my sister Loli was a good dancer in the dance club.

During the first spring in New York, Angel joined the Cubs Scouts, which met at the church auditorium every week. He wore his blue uniform and eventually earned stickers which I got to sew on specific parts of this uniform. He had to complete many tasks which my parents had to agree and sign in his workbook. Angel was very enthusiastic about his club and often talked about joining the military when he grew up. The Cubs Scouts tasks had replaced some of Angel's desire to control the TV. He spent time building stuff and completing projects to earn awards.

TV continued to be Loli's favorite pastime. She knew all the schedules and who were the actors and the stories behind every show. Loli was only a year and eight months younger than me, but I always saw her as much younger. She was the prettiest among us. Her resemblance to Mami was very clear. They both had the same type of nose and small lips that looked painted pink all the time. She had slanted small eyes and thin long lashes. Sometimes people called her *flaca* because she was low weight and had thin legs. I always told her that she was the smartest of the kids, but she never believed me, and I seldom saw her study or read, although she always came home with good grades. She is the only one of my siblings whose birth I do not remember. But I do remember telling my mother that I was tickled to have a sister to be able to play and love. I continued to say this after Angel was born and became a demanding toddler.

I remember that Loli cried every time there was a sad episode on TV. I think that her favorite show was *Bewitched*. She got into the plot of that story very much, and she also clapped and cheered for exciting scenes. Sometimes she made such ruckus while watching TV that the adults had to reprimand her for being loud. Whenever there was a scary scene, she would scream along as well. She also enjoyed the *Monster Family* so she could scream every time there was a scary scene. One night, we were allowed to watch TV late, and the show began with a monster's hand coming out of the earth and taking the letters off the title into the ground. She screamed the entire show. "It is time for bed," said Daddy after hearing her loudest screams. We were not allowed to watch that show again unless we watched it on the sneak on a Friday night or on school break.

It was not until Christmas break of '71 that my siblings and I discovered that there were no TV shows past certain time at night. We were so disappointed since that night, both of our parents had fallen asleep and left us watching TV in the living room. At first, we began to move the antenna around and changed the channels, thinking that was the issue. Some channels were playing the national anthem, and we thought that was strange.

"That's unfair," I whined under my breath. One by one, we went to bed disappointed and silently so that our parents would not wake up and notice we had stayed up late watching TV.

THE NEW SCHOOL

At the beginning of October of '71, my siblings and I were transferred to the new bilingual school in the Bronx. It was an elementary school located in a different neighborhood from where we lived. The change to a better learning environment was felt immediately. At the dinner table, we shared with our parents how we had all experienced a nicer time at school. The teachers all spoke Spanish, and we attended special English classes where the language was being taught to us.

Ody remained at the old school for the rest of that school year. Loli, Angel, and I rode the bus every day to attend our new school. The bus ride took about twenty minutes, and upon our arrival at school, we all waited in the big room at the entrance that was used for various purposes: gym, lunch, and auditorium. Every morning, our teachers would come for us in the big room, and we all lined up in size places and followed to our respective classrooms. These teachers were able to pronounce our names properly. They smiled when calling our names and did not make mockery of anyone's non-English sounding name.

My teacher was Ms. Rivera, and she taught fifth grade. Later that year, she got married and became Mrs. Jacobowitz. She was originally from Puerto Rico but came to this country while still a baby. She was very pretty and had a very pointy nose. She wore very tight jeans with bell bottoms. She also wore various colors of very tight turtlenecks most of the time. She spoke softly and was very patient when any of the students could not pronounce a word in English. When she spoke Spanish, I often had to figure out in my head what she said. I could not tell her that her sentences were not correct. Although she was much nicer than the nuns back in the old country, she was still my teacher, and I would not want to make her angry. Whenever she got upset at a student, her ears got red, and her nose jiggled like Daddy's nose when he got annoyed.

During the spring term, schoolwork became more interesting. There were new teachers who helped our original teachers, and there were changes made. Loli got a new teacher who she often spoke about at dinner chat. Angel met his first male teacher, and that made him happy. My teacher continued to be Mrs. Jacobowitz, and she was very active in school. Other teachers often asked for her help and for her materials. She had an assistant who helped the students who were having a hard time. By the spring, I had become known for reading a lot and for helping my classmates with math problems. I also enjoyed history and was specifically interested in learning about the United States' history and culture.

I was very excited when my teacher told us that during the spring semester, we were going to be introduced to reading long books. One of the changes that had occurred at our new school that spring semester was the addition of a library. Students were told we would independently be reading a different book every month. We would take notes and answer questions for each book we read. That assignment would be part of the final grade in language class. I was thrilled to be able to go to the school library. It was a small room with some books on small shelves and a long reading table at the center. The walls were decorated with bright posters of books. The lights were glistening. Just like the rest of the school, there were no windows in this library, and a vent blew over my head no matter where I sat at the long reading table. The teacher assistant used to take small groups to the library so students could select the book to read that month.

One day, when my reading group returned to class, the teacher asked each one to tell why we selected the book we had chosen. That day, I stood up and explained in Spanish why I had selected *Las Aventuras del Mio Sid*. I said that I selected that book because it was one of the books in my father's book trunk back at home in the Dominican Republic. I never had a chance to read it while I was there. So when I saw it at the library, it made me very happy. My teacher approached me and motioned to me to hand her my book. She read the review in the back and commented, "Esto es difícil," as she wrinkled her face. She got close to me and said that I would not be able to understand that reading, and she suggested that I select an easier book. I could see her nose flickering as it turned red.

That day, on my way home on the bus, my teacher's words replayed in my head and made me perturbed and disappointed. I continued to think about this for the rest of the day and perhaps the remainder of the week. Images returned of the day Mami went to register us at the old school and instead of seventh grade, I ended in fifth grade because the school counselor said that would be a better option for me since I did not speak English. Mami explained it many times, but I did not understand how that was a good idea to place me back because of language. So I promised myself to give the best of myself at school and "learn good English" like my abuelo suggested before we left our homeland.

Las Aventuras del Mio Cid was a Spanish classic story about the adventures of a knight during Medieval times. I had the intention to read that book when I was in Abuelo's farm, but did not get a chance to read it before I left. The other books I read at Abuelo's had taken me a long time to read because they were complicated. Every time we were on vacation from school, my aunt Isabel used to come and pick us up from the boarding school, and we would spend time at my abuelo's farm in the countryside. That farm was in the south of the country in the province of Bani, which was about three hours west from the school in Boca Chica. During our visits to the farm, I read Dante's *Divine Comedy*, and while I enjoyed these long poems, the voices, and chants in the *Inferno* part gave me nightmares. Although I did not understand some of the books I read, I was able to get some idea of what the messages were. "Every story has a message," I remember Daddy saying when I began to read long books at age 6, and "each story teaches a lesson," he also said. Because I read every day, I got very good at discovering many of the messages. Sometimes I had to read it twice before I saw it. The first time that I read *Don Quixote de la Mancha*, I was nine years old. Although I laughed at many of the episodes described in that story, overall, I did not get to appreciate the book until I read it again in college. Reading became a safe space for me as I waited for my parents to send for my siblings and me. Later, as I learned the ways to this new home in New York, reading continued to be my safe space, where I could tune out many distractions and deprivations imposed by poverty.

At the end of the month, when I handed my book report to my teacher, I felt confident that I had done a good job. I had placed special effort in presenting a good report to her and even added a drawing of the knight in the story engaged in a battle. I loved drawing, and Mami had bought me a set of pastel drawing pencils and a drawing pad that I enjoyed using. I received a good grade on my report, and the teacher even posted my project on the board of excellent work for the month. From that time on, I decided not to be bothered by what unnecessary criticism I would get from adults and focus on what I liked to do instead. I disliked when adults would assume that I could not do a task and most of the time made it my goal to prove them wrong. When kids would challenge me, then I set out to become better than them and show them with actions how wrong they were. *Testadura* or hard-headed was a word I often heard from my abuela Abi when she would catch me modifying any of her commands. I never understood why I needed to follow all instructions to the precise wish of the commander when I could use my creativity and skills to accomplish the task to exceed the expectations.

Even when I was very young, I was highly competitive and enjoyed winning over those who doubted my abilities. "Pride is a sin," had once warned the mother superior at the boarding school. She thought that my competitive behavior was wrong. Although I did not question her, I decided to read about pride and found some examples in the Bible. It was then I decided that competitiveness could not be such a bad thing even for someone as simple as me. Besides, my abuelo had said that one needed to have pride in their work. "Do the best possible job all the time if no one was getting hurt in the process," said my abuelo when I approached him about pride. Daddy had also said a variation of Abuelo's words many times. Mami agreed that was a good thing as well to have pride in one's work and always encouraged us to do our work well the first time around.

At an early age, I learned that not all things were up for competition. I became aware that there were elements of life which just happened without any control, nor desire. As the spring arrived, I continued to be one of the taller girls in fifth grade. Some of the girls in my class had grown during the past months and had moved on to the back of the line. "You're still the same size," said some girls when I remained the third one toward the back of the line in the school hallway, bright with colorful charts and decorations made of paper flowers. The shortest one in our class continued to be my friend, Martha. Although she had grown a little since October, she never got as tall as the rest of the girls in class. Martha had pretty dark brown curls and a beautiful smile. "Somos jirafas," we giggled as we measured our long eyelashes in front of the lavatory mirror and mocked each other, saying they were long enough like those of a giraffe. Martha was waiting to turn thirteen so that she could get braces like the other kids with teeth that were not lined. When two girls mocked her teeth as they left the bathroom, she shared with me that as a small child, she used to suck her thumb, and that made her teeth crooked. My sister Ody had the same issues and needed braces when she became of age. "Ignore them," I said as we headed back to math class.

I enjoyed Martha's company, and we were both good at math. Her parents were born in Puerto Rico and had sent her back to the island to live with her grandparents for a few years. Martha and I shared similar stories about our grandparents and many cousins. Like my parents, Martha's mother was also very protective. Her only outing was school and church. Her mother worked long hours at a big store, and Martha's grandmother took care of her in the afternoons after school. We were both attempting to learn English and adapt to this new land.

By the end of fifth-grade year, I learned a little English and was able to read some sentences, advertisements, and articles in one of the newspapers that Mrs. Jacobowitz brought to class occasionally.

"Good job," said my teacher to express how happy she was with my progress in the new language.

I made new friends in my class and was close to some of the kids in the six-grade class as well. I joined clubs in school and was one of the top students in my grade. My teacher selected me to be one of the students to participate in the overnight trip to the capital of the United States, Washington, DC, and my closest friends were also asked to go. Since it was an honor to be asked to go on this trip, Mami and Daddy allowed me to participate. "Puedes ir a la excursión," they said when I read the permission slip and letter of invitation to them. Later that weekend, I found my parents discussing the cost of my trip to Washington, DC.

Toward the last weeks of school, my classmates and I went off on the bus trip to DC. It was my first trip out of New York state since arriving the year before. On that trip, I discovered fast food called McDonald's. I loved the vanilla shake and the cheeseburger with fries. The burger had something called pickles in it and a combination of mayonnaise and mustard sauce. My friends placed a layer of fries in between the burger and the bun, so did I. What an awesome food that was and wondered out loud among my friends if this type of food was to be served at school. "What a good idea that would be," they agreed. I had finally discovered my preferred American food.

Visiting the national monuments and walking up the steps to the Capitol made me very happy. The Washington Monument reminded me of a smaller version of a similar monument in the city of Santo Domingo. There were flowers called tulips, which I had never noticed before. The pink blossom trees were fascinating.

My friends and I took pictures by the Washington Monument with a little camera Daddy had provided me. There were only twenty-four pictures in that film. Only two other kids had cameras, so we took turns taking pictures of everyone on the trip, as suggested by our teacher. She also suggested we take notes of our trip so we could write a report about it upon returning to school. Thanks to those notes, I learned to document special events in my life. Many of the memories I carry with me are based on my notes throughout the years.

The last day of school, I learned that my teacher, Mrs. Jacobowitz, would follow us to the next grade, and that comforted me much. I tried to hug her, but she said she was not allowed to hug me back. So I just grabbed on to her arm as I used to hug my abuelo. Her perfume tickled my nose, but I did not mind this time. I had come to admire my teacher and enjoyed her dedication to all her students. I watched her deal with students in difficult situations and how she solved many problems among some of my classmates. She continued to speak softly and was intentional about her approach to each one of her students' needs and progress. A school year that began with knots in my stomach and full of uncertainty had turned out to be one of discovery and hope. I looked forward to moving on to six-grade again and was sure this time I would not be returning to a lower grade. At my new school, I continued to overcome the challenges of learning a new language and culture and planned to maintain good grades and participate in many school activities.

THE BUS RIDE TO SCHOOL
AND THE SNOW

Every morning since my sister Loli, my brother Angel, and I were transferred to the new school in the fall of '71, we had taken the yellow bus in front of our old school. Ody remained at the old school. Her grade was not taught at the new school, which was designated for students who did not speak English and who had arrived from other countries around the world. Papi dropped us off at the bus stop before he hopped on his own bus to his new job at a factory. The bus came for us at 7:15 sharp, and if any kid was late, their parents would have to drop them off on their own. Loli and Angel sat next to me on the bus during the first week. Later, they made friends their own age and traveled to and from school together with their new buddies.

The days began to get cold in the mornings as October kicked in with windy days. The first time I wore a sweater made me feel happy. There was no need to wear a sweater where I came from. The sweater was my favorite color blue, and it had big blue buttons as well. Many of my outfits were blue because Mami said that color was very becoming on me. With the colder days, the windows on the bus were closed, and days later, the heat rose from underneath the seats. Sometimes the heat was too hot on my legs, and I had to stretch them in fear of getting burned. On rainy days, the windows on the bus got very foggy. It was hilarious that my brother Angel's glasses also fogged up.

Angel wore glasses from the time he was two years old. He had suffered eye issues as a toddler and was subjected to two corrective eye surgeries while we still lived in the Dominican Republic. He looked like a mini professor when he wore his tiny bowtie to Sunday mass. Sometimes when we played in the park, other kids mocked him and called him four eyes. Each time I noticed that he was being bothered, "Leave him alone," I intervened and eventually made those kids pay for their mockery. As the older child among my siblings, I felt the obligation to defend them from everyone whom I thought would harm them. Many times, I would just pinch a kid so hard, they twisted in pain. Other times I stepped on their toes or made them trip as they passed by. Once, I placed a thumbtack on the bus seat and watched kids jump in pain. Bullies were made to pay for things they did to my siblings. "You asked for it," I would mumble quietly under my breath. I always waited for the right moment as adults were not witnessing my acts of being mischievous. I got very good at exercising patience and waiting for the right moment. It made me very frustrated when I was unable to defend my siblings from other kids or even adults.

At school, I was part of the soprano group in the school choir. I loved the music teacher because she reminded me of my abuela Abi, but much nicer. She patiently taught us how to read music and how to support each other's voices. The first songs she taught us were about Puerto Rico, and mostly written by Rafael Hernandez. That was also the name of our new school. We celebrated the discovery of the island sometime in November. In history class, we learned about the history of Puerto Rico, and in Spanish class, we read some poems that celebrated the *jibaro* and an important river on that island, which was reflected in a long poem by Julia de Burgos. I had to memorize and recite part of the poem for class, so it has remains in my mind forever.

That fall, I also learned about a holiday called Thanksgiving. In music class I learned new songs to celebrate this special holiday, and some of the younger students were part of a small play and dressed as Native North American people and Pilgrims.

When the feast of Thanksgiving arrived, I had to help Mami prepare some of the many dishes for that day. She bought a big turkey and stuffed it with an apple and a big onion. I had never eaten turkey before and had never seen a big bird like that other than at the zoo when we saw an ostrich. Mami began to roast the big bird early in the morning, and the entire home, along with the rest of the building smelled like roast turkey. The neighbors were also roasting turkey. I did not enjoy that smell nor liked the taste of turkey later when we sat down for dinner. While trying to ignore the smell of that bird, I picked at the meat that evening and focused on eating the rest of the delicious feast.

The nicer part of that holiday was the long weekend we enjoyed at home as a family. Daddy and Mami were also off that Friday and the weekend, and we played many table games together and again told more stories about the time we were separated from each other. Angel usually beat us at Monopoly, and Daddy was the best at Dominos. "I won!" they yelled each time.

At the dinner table, several times that weekend, Daddy tried to explain the reasons why we had to be uprooted from our homeland: the downfall of one government after another, the US invasion of 1965, the dismantling of the sugar industry that led to Daddy's loss of his nice job. Daddy had worked in *Central Boca Chica* in the payroll department. He enjoyed his job in the sugar industry, and he was well respected and efficient. He got to wear a tie and carry a briefcase to work. In Boca Chica, we owned our own house by the beach. I attended the Catholic school since I was four, and it later became our boarding school when my parents came to the US to pave the way before they sent for us to join them in New York. "Vinimos a trabajar," Daddy said as he caressed my brother's head and went on to explain why he worked so hard all the time.

When my siblings and I asked questions about his current jobs in New York, Daddy was not as enthusiastic as usual, although he often turned his stories into jokes and learning points. When we first arrived, Daddy worked at a factory and sold home products via a catalogue. Sometimes he helped his friend across the street with his grocery store duties and later became the manager for that grocery store. Daddy worked all the time, but was always available to spend time with the family when he was off from work. Sometimes when he came home late at night, I watched him quietly kiss each one of us on our foreheads and say a prayer before leaving our bedroom.

Mami spent all her time after work taking care of us and the home. She took pride in keeping a gleaming home where the bathroom was glistening, and the pots were all bright and polished as well. Every Saturday morning, she made my sister Loli and I deep clean the kitchen appliances and walls, scrub the floors, dust all the furniture and windows, and arrange the closets. We took turns to ensure all the work was done before noon so we could have the rest of the day to play and do other things. After completing those tasks, Mami would inspect everything to make sure the work was done to perfection. She would even inspect under the beds and behind the toilet. "Come here, you!" Mami would interrupt us when we were playing and while grabbing my sister and me by the ear. She was very stern about doing things right the first time around, so I mostly tried to complete my tasks to her liking so that she would not punish me for missing anything.

Although Mami was a taskmaster, she was also very attentive to our well-being and manners. She noticed the smallest scratch or ailment. She would place the covers over each one of us and bless our foreheads followed by a kiss and a hug before she shut the lights off every night. Mami would spend many nights by our side when any of the children were ill. Every morning, there was warm breakfast served at the table before we left for school.

That first fall in New York, daylight continued to get shorter as the air got brisker. When we got on the bus in the mornings, it was mostly foggy, and it got dark again soon after we got home from school. One day, I asked my fifth-grade teacher about this phenomenon, she said that the winter was near, and the days got shorter as December arrived. She explained that the reason why many cultures celebrated festival of lights in the winter was because winters were mostly void of natural light and there was little sun during the entire winter. I understood that the celebrations were meant to bring some brightness to gloomy days.

Shortly after Thanksgiving, while on the bus on our way to school one morning, I saw snowflakes for the first time. It made me very happy to finally see snow and noticed how they floated around as the bus moved by. Some flakes attached themselves to the windows on the bus as if they needed a ride somewhere. I was fascinated with the intricate shapes each flake had.

The kids on the bus made lots of noise and sang a song unfamiliar to me. They also seemed happy, and my friend Martha told me that later when school ended, we would see a lot of snow accumulated on the ground and to be careful not to slip when walking. I did not understand her warning until we left school, and walking through the fluffy white stuff was very difficult. I had to balance myself not to fall as some other kids did. On our walk home from the bus, kids were also making snowballs and throwing them at each other. I was not familiar with that practice and was so cold that I just watched and accelerated my pace home to stay away from the flying snowballs.

That evening at dinner time, the topic of conversation was our first snow. Each one of us had a story to tell, and Daddy shared how the bus he was riding home had come to a complete stop because it was not able to go up the hill. The passengers had to get off and walk the rest of the way to catch the other bus that went across town. That night, he arrived home later than usual due to the bus mishap during the first snow of the season.

Mami had a simple story because she took the subway home, and there was no interruption for her. "Hace frio." She was shivering when she arrived to pick us up from the cousins' place and rushed home to boil ginger tea with honey for all of us to have before she prepared dinner.

Angel's story was the funniest of all because when he decided to bend down to pick up snow and roll a snowball, his glasses fell into the snow, and for a moment, he was not able to find them. His little friend found them, and when he put them back on, they were all foggy and was unable to see properly. "I can't see!" I heard him yell as he slipped and fell.

Loli and I did not have much to share except we were cold, and our shoes were slippery and wet when we walked home from the bus stop. That day, I wore a dress to school, and although I had thick tights on, that did not help in the frosty and wet snow. Every step home from the bus made a crackling sound, and snow got into my shoes.

Ody shared that she tasted the snow and made believe it was tasteless ice cream. Upon hearing her, Mami admonished her about the germs she must have placed into her mouth by doing that. I tried not to get caught rolling my eyes about Mami's comments.

It was a little late by the time we finished our dinner, so we had to get ready for bed and prepare our outfits for the next morning. I did not sleep well the night of the first snow because there were loud noises coming from the streets. There was the sound of metal being dragged and chains rolling, and lots of loud banging noise outside. All that noise kept me awake most of the night.

The sound of dragging chains reminded me of an earlier experience when my family's house in Boca Chica Beach was surrounded by US Marines during the US occupation of 1965. For many days, the US Marines went about their daily activities, which disrupted the way of life of our community. Early morning quiet was disrupted by the sounds of dragging chains followed by marching boots and synchronized repetition of words I did not understand. Once, when I got on a chair and peeked out the window in my room, I saw a big army tank rolling down the road and followed by many soldiers marching behind the big tank. I covered my ears and was scared. My entire body was shaking when I went to hide under the bedsheet.

By daylight, after the snowfall, the streets had turned into a muddy slush. There were piles of dirty snow at each corner of the streets. The day after that first snow, the beautiful white flakes had disappeared, and the sun was bright and the air colder than the day before. Subsequent snowfalls came down in different quantities throughout that winter.

Although I enjoyed each snowfall less each time, it was always amazing to see how beautiful the flakes were and the details in them as they stuck to the windows on the bus as it slowly moved toward and from our school. Each time, the kids on the bus made such noise and became alarmed at each snow fall and sang the same song, which I did not yet understand.

Although Mami had bought each one of us snow boots, hats, gloves, scarves, and heavy sweaters, I still felt very cold each time it snowed. By the end of the winter, I had become tired of the flakes falling from the sky and the happiness and excitement I felt during the first snow had slowly disappeared over time. I came to know that the cold and dark winters were not my preferred season. That first winter in New York felt endless and bothersome.

As a skinny kid, I spent much of the time shivering and wearing multiple layers of clothes, which made me tired. I tried hard to reconcile having to learn the new ways of life in New York and the memories of the warm blue sea at our old house and the large green trees at Abuelo's farmland all at once, trying to keep somewhat happy. The winter was void of natural light and the familiar tropical smells of mango, banana, guava, sugar cane, and earth. My school had no windows. The bright lights that were always on in every corner of the school made my eyes tired as the school day progressed. One of my favorite school times was the ride home when I was able to sit by the school bus window and stare outside while ignoring the loud noise made by most of the kids.

At night, when I lay awake in my bed, the smell of burning metal and coal in the distance tickled my throat and clogged my nose. I also heard firetruck sirens and wondered why this town, called the Bronx, was burning. During the afternoons, as I stared out the window on the ride home from school, I noticed several burned buildings. Every week, there were new burned buildings, and I often wondered why that was a common thing here. I questioned where the people who lived there had gone. As I got older, I learned to reconcile the reasons behind the Bronx burning and felt very upset about the social ills faced by the people who lived in the area. The thoughts of burned buildings reminded me of an old memory when parts of the capital city of Santo Domingo had burned stone buildings after the invasion of 1965. The difference here was that there was no political conflict that I was aware of, and life seemed to continue to happen as usual although many more buildings were burning all the time.

Years later, when I did a project for the public relations class in high school, I learned about some of the reasons why the Bronx was burning in the 1970s. I read in some news reports that the lack of civil engagement from some members of the community created the conditions for buildings to become vulnerable to criminal behavior by its own inhabitants. I also read about the level of greed exerted by some "slumlords," who had provoked some fires due to the lack of maintenance to the buildings that they rented to an influx of black and brown tenants. During my research, I also interviewed a community activist who believed that some landlords had fires set on purpose to collect insurance money.

Amid many of the challenges that were part of my family's lives both at the old country as well as in the new land, we continued to maintain a reasonable, united, and loving homelife. Often, when I asked Daddy why buildings were burning or why there were gangs in the streets or people without jobs just wandering around the streets all day, he was not able to answer but promised to find out for me. He never had a clear answer about the social issues when questioned at the dinner table and tried to turn those serious conversations into more easygoing topics about happier things. Daddy claimed that people should focus on the little things in life instead of worrying about world problems we could not resolve. He said that prayers alleviate many of the ills in the world and that God had a purpose for all things big and small. Our dinner conversations were lively and often full of laughter as we all tried to talk at once until Mami would continuously shush everyone down, and Daddy and the kids quickly ignored her "shush" and laughed again and again over silly things both big and small.

With time, I learned to find answers to social issues outside of home discussions. I read and asked other adults about dire issues in our society. After all, my homelife was a happy place, and my parents sheltered us from the chaos that reigned outside our apartment. They offered us protection, food, and shelter from all the sad stories we encountered once we set foot outside our home. Their demonstrations of love, easygoing attitude, and low-drama demeanor made it easier for my siblings and me to withstand the pressures and chaos of the outside world where we lived.

WHEN PAPI BECAME DADDY

The fall of '71 was very interesting. The trees changed colors. As time progressed, they all became yellow and orange. A few remained green for the rest of the year. Some trees were red and even rust brown. I had never seen trees with those colors nor behave that way. On Saturdays, when Mami took us to the park, we played in the piles of leaves, making little mounds and then jumping into them and throwing the leaves up in the air to see them fly around with the wind. Mami was not too happy with those games because she said the leaves were dirty. They must have been dirty since I sneezed constantly, and my eyes teared up most of the time when we played among the leaves those days. Even with all the discomfort in breathing, I continued to play in the mounds of leaves and helped my siblings bury themselves in them.

Saturday afternoons were the only time we were allowed to leave the home other than school time and church day. My sister Loli, Angel, and I were lucky to have been transferred to a different school during the first week of October. Every morning, we got to take the bus and ride to a different neighborhood with a busload of loud kids.

I noticed how the trees had changed colors during a bus ride to school on a windy morning. There were leaves blown about as the bus drove through the underpass at 161st Street. And as the bus exited on the other side of the Grand Concourse, the pile of leaves seemed to follow our path. At first, I thought the trees were all getting sick. That evening, when I mentioned it at the dinner table, Papi explained that the trees were not getting sick; rather they changed colors at this time of year because it was the autumn season. He added that gradually they will lose all their leaves to welcome the winter season. That night, as I lay in bed bright awake due to my excessive coughing, I wondered how strange it was that if winters were cold, the trees would be naked precisely at that time of year. I had heard that winters in New York were very cold. I wondered then why the trees would lose their leaves and how they protected themselves during the cold season.

It was also during the fall that we celebrated the most fun but strange holiday. The last Saturday in October, Mami took my siblings and me shopping for costumes. She explained that on that Sunday after church, we would go out with those costumes on. She said that this was a holiday for pumpkins, witches, and goblins. She added that all children dressed in costumes and went out to collect candy at the neighbors' homes. And as she mentioned the word *witches*, she made the sign of the cross. While at a store called Alexanders, we were each able to select a mask to wear for that day only. My brother, Angel, had a hard time selecting a mask that would suit Mami's budget. All the ones he picked exceeded the amount of money she had available. Angel always wanted the most expensive things whenever we went shopping. He cried when Mami could not afford the things he selected. Loli was usually happy with whatever she got. I was picky and selective whenever we went shopping, but this time, I thought the holiday was silly so the mask was not important to me, and I cannot even remember what I chose.

That Sunday afternoon, on Halloween, Mami took us around to knock on all the doors at our building. Everyone opened their door and placed a piece of candy in each of our baskets that were shaped like a pumpkin. I had carefully written our names on each basket before leaving our home. As we knocked on each apartment door, it occurred to me that I never noticed there were so many homes in our building. We lived on the fourth floor, and there were two more levels above ours and one apartment under the ground in a location called the basement.

I wondered how many people lived in each apartment and how large the rooms were inside. Our elderly cousins lived on the first floor, and their apartment wrapped around the corner. The people who lived next door to our cousins had become friendly with us because their younger daughter, who was a few years older than me, often picked my siblings and I from the school bus and walked us to the cousins' home, where we waited for Mami to return from work. The girl mostly spoke English and just a few words in Spanish. She said she was born in the Bronx and had never visited Puerto Rico, where her parents were born. She attended high school and said she was preparing to celebrate her sixteenth birthday in the spring. Her sister was older and very pretty and wore tall platform shoes that made a lot of noise when she walked rapidly across the living room hardwood floor. She said that a place called a boiler room was underneath their apartment when I told her that Mami did not allow us to walk so hard in case we disturb the neighbors below us. The girls each had their own room and shared a bathroom separate from their parents. That Halloween these girls invited us in for a little while, and they gave us extra candy to take home. That day the girls taught us how to dance American-style disco music. Their mother was very nice to us as well. She enjoyed talking to Mami every time they saw each other.

When we came home from collecting candy, Mami asked us to stay in the living room while she prepared dinner. She turned the TV on for us and told us to count our pieces of candy. We were only allowed to have two pieces "only after dinner," she said repeatedly. That suggestion did not work at all. I ate too many pieces of candy while we were walking around and ate some more while Mami prepared the food.

I gagged at the thought of food and had a hard time eating dinner that day. With just a few exceptions, I was not too fond of cooked food. I preferred cheese and crackers and lots of fruit. My favorite food was *mangú*, mashed green plantains, and fried eggs, but that was only made for breakfast on weekends. I also enjoyed avocados and mangoes, but since moving to New York, we had not eaten any. To me, most of the food in New York had a different smell and taste. Even bananas tasted different, and the smell of them was faint. I missed the fresh smell of fruit back at *Abuelo's* farm. Mami often complained about my sisters and me because we were picky eaters. Angel ate everything without a problem; the three girls were finicky about most foods.

That evening, Papi came home just in time for dinner. Although it was Sunday, he was now a salesperson during his spare time. He sold home products from a catalogue and carried a heavy black briefcase as large as a suitcase. Every weekend, he visited people's homes to make presentations for a company called Stanley. He referred to Stanley so often that at first, I thought it was a person and wondered why Mr. Stanley needed my dad's help to sell his things. Mr. Stanley was taking our papi away during the little time he could spend being around us.

My siblings and I enjoyed being around Papi. He was fun and loving. He played with us all the time. We climbed on Papi all at once and pulled his ears, his nose, his fingers. Papi loved to get his back scratched and his hair combed. One day we dressed him up with some of Mami's jewelry. We put pearl strings around his neck and clipped on dangling earrings and bracelets on his wrist. Papi fell asleep by the time we were done decorating him, so we left him alone to rest on the couch.

That day on Halloween, while we sat around the dinner table chatting about family issues and projects, Ody announced that from now on, we would have to learn how to pronounce all our names as they sounded in English. Since Papi's middle name was Dario and most people in our family called him by that name instead of his first name, Angel, Ody suggested we all begin to call Papi, Daddy. Afterall, he was our daddy.

By the end of the fall, Ody was the only one of us who was speaking English somewhat fluently. She had learned the new language quickly and was doing very well in her English-only school. She was a happy six-year-old in first grade. Ody learned English fluently by the end of that school year. Later, she also learned American Sign Language from a young neighbor whose entire family was hearing impaired. In high school, she learned French. As a grown-up, Ody became a successful certified court interpreter in Spanish/English.

Ody's suggestion was welcomed by all of us including Papi, so we agreed to call him by his new name, Daddy. He continued to be a jolly person even with his new name, and soon all our friends and cousins referred to him as Daddy. Daddy was a nice person to everyone he knew. Around the time Papi became Daddy, we all dropped the Spanish diminutive at the end of each of our names, and we became Angela, Yolanda, Angel, and Odelis became Ody. With time, we continued to modify our names, and I became Angie, while Yolanda became Loli. That very first fall in New York, unknowingly, we were already becoming Americans.

MAMI

It wasn't until Mami had grandchildren that she allowed herself to laugh about just anything like the rest of us. While growing up, I remember Mami being very loving but very stringent. Although she had a beautiful smile with perfectly lined and shaped white teeth, she was often pensive and serious and would not join Daddy's laughter with us at the dinner table. She would stare into thin air as if searching into the future and foreseeing some type of catastrophic event for which she had to prepare and protect our family. Years later, after my grandmother Abi and Daddy had passed away and I spent some time alone with Mami, she began to tell me details about her hard-lived childhood.

When we were growing up, Mami always hinted about her hard life as a child. "I had a difficult childhood," she often said but never gave us any details until we were grown up. Mami's father passed away when she was only two years old. My abuela, Abi, as we all called her, was still pregnant with her third child when her husband suddenly passed away while on a business trip. Abi became a very angry woman who displayed her frustrations on her children by beating them unconscious at times. Abi never remarried nor was known to have any social life. She moved herself and her little young children to a large city in search of better opportunities. Mami's older brother, Ramon, was also very authoritarian and overprotective with his two younger sisters. Although he was only five years older than Mami, he became the man of the house once Abi became a widow.

Mami always said that she would have loved to have the opportunity to study at the university in her hometown, but Abi could not afford even the uniform nor the books for her to finish high school. Her financial circumstances only allowed her to complete a high school equivalency degree for young ladies. At that time, there were clear distinctions as to the career choices appropriate for girls. Mami studied home economics at the institute for young ladies, for which she received a certificate of completion. For as long as I can remember, that certificate hung next to Daddy's bookkeeping certificate on a hallway wall at our home.

During one of our lengthy conversations, Mami told me that she began to work at an early age so she could help with the family finances. She worked at the local theater at the tickets window. On days when the theater was closed, she embroidered and crocheted baby outfits for expecting mothers. She said that she would get commission pay for that type of work, and that allowed her to pay for her school uniform and materials.

By the time I was thirteen years old, Mami had taught me how to run a household, care for a sick person, and was introducing me to home finances. I was made in charge of taking the money to the bank and depositing it for her. As her first child, she made me her assistant.

Mami controlled every move in our household and somehow managed to find out who was up to what all the time. She used to say that she was nosy about our business for our own safety. Whenever possible, she intervened either physically or with prayers. Mami was the unyielding disciplinarian at home and often used her chancleta or her knuckles to let her position be known. Mami's noogies would make me dizzy. She was quick and sharp, and no one would escape her wrath when she had to discipline or defend her children.

When my sister Loli came of age, Mami trained her to do the same housework as me. And by the time we were young teenagers, Mami took a back seat to running the chores for the household. My sister Loli and I were responsible for cooking, maintaining the home clean, the laundry, and taking care of our two younger siblings.

By the time I turned thirteen, Mami worked long hours at night cleaning offices in Manhattan, and a few years later, my grandmother Abi moved on to her own apartment, first to a building around the corner from us, and years after that, she moved to Brooklyn near her older son. Mami slept while we were in school, and by the time we returned, she was getting ready for work. So Loli and I remained to run the household while Daddy came home from work. Every night, Daddy would get up in the middle of the night to go wait for Mami at the train station by 2:00 a.m. I often heard him quietly leave and return about half an hour later with Mami. He then took a nap until it was time for him to get up again to head on to his own job. "Dios bendiga," said Daddy every morning before leaving for work. He would make the sign of the cross on each one of our foreheads and quietly head out to have a productive day.

Mami would then prepare hot breakfast for us and ensure we did not miss the bus to school. We were all out the door by 7:00 a.m. We were never allowed to stay home, even when we were sick. Mami said our only real job was school, and we had to take it seriously. After we all left on the school bus, I assume Mami came back home and finally went to bed to rest after a long night of work as a cleaning lady for large offices in Midtown Manhattan.

When it was time for me to attend college, Mami, in her limited way, supported all my efforts and encouraged me to go away to another state. She often spoke about how proud she was of all her children and how much God had blessed her by having smart offspring. Mami would always make sure we learned proper manners and that we knew how to behave in any and every crowd. I watched as other ladies she knew, including the older cousins, would sometimes criticize her for exhibiting and focusing so much on manners. They would mock the fact that Mami insisted that we always eat dinner at a properly set table, that we exhibited respect for people and property, and that we spoke only proper academic Spanish. Mami hoped and prayed that someday we would all be successful and honorable citizens of the United States.

Years later, when I returned home from college for my first break, Mami complained how some of the professionals at her job mocked her and called her a liar for saying that she had a daughter who attended Wellesley College. I told Mami not to worry about those men because they were racists who could not understand and admit that not only their children could become high achievers. At Wellesley, I had already begun to study about the big ills of this society: discrimination, classism, sexism, and racism.

At church, Mami was well respected by other parishioners. She was an active member of the lady's prayer group, and she read at mass on Sundays. She organized collections for the needy and was part of the parish council. The priests and nuns trusted her with many tasks in church, and when my sister Loli married in Santo Domingo years later, Mami invited the pastor to officiate the wedding. My parents paid his way so he could visit and perform the ceremony there. Mami took care of the arrangements with the church over there.

Mami also became friends with Sister Marie, who was like a mentor for Mami as she navigated this new country to us. Sister Marie did not wear a habit and would take my siblings and me to the neighborhood pool during the summer. I remember the first time I saw Sister Marie in a bathing suit. The nuns I was used to at the boarding school were so strict about wearing their habit and not allowing any parts of their body to be seen that I thought nuns had no flesh under all those clothes. I had imagined that nuns only had extremities and a face. Meeting Sister Marie and having her become Mami's friend felt very refreshing yet awkward at once. Sister Marie was more modern and in tune with pop culture than Mami. Although she was older than Mami, Sister Marie was also less traditional than our young mother. Sister Marie taught my siblings and me how to swim in the large pool and dive from the trampoline. Once, when Mami came along with us, she was so scared to see us dive that she closed her eyes out of fear. Sister Marie also introduced me to rock and roll as well as to disco and pop music. When charity dances were organized at church, Sister Marie was the first one to arrive and dance and the last one to leave the party. I learned my first disco steps from her during my first summer camp job, where she was the director. She loved all types of music and knew all the new steps of the moment.

When I turned thirteen, my pediatrician referred me to a teenage specialist at the clinic. Because Mami was so conservative, she was very distraught about that suggestion and discussed it at length with Sister Marie. After a long conversation, which details I do not remember completely, Sister Marie was finally able to convince Mami that it was very normal for her children to grow up and for her to allow them to flourish and thrive in all aspects of life. It made me very happy that Sister Marie was Mami's friend.

For many years while I was growing up, I remember Mami holding two jobs at the same time. Unlike Daddy, she rarely spoke about her day at work when asked. Occasionally, she would just remind us that she was doing this type of work so that none of her children would ever have to because they were being given the opportunities to study that she never had. By the time Mami became a grandmother many years later, she began to ease up and smile more often. She took on to joking around just like Daddy. She was proud of her four professional, hardworking, and respected children. "Hemos hecho un buen trabajo, viejo," she would often weigh up with Daddy as she talked about how their hard work and focus as parents had turned into good outcomes for their children.

Years later, as a mother, I have tried to emulate some of my own mother's good qualities. She was attentive to detail about her children's well-being, loving, when necessary, strict about raising productive and caring individuals, and fastidious about our happiness. When my child was born, my mother was the only person who I trusted to care for my baby when I returned to work two months after her birth. As a grandmother, Mami showed tender loving care for my daughter, and I have many times told her how grateful I am for having her in my life.

WHEN THE THREE KINGS
WERE REPLACED

"Apúrate!" said Mami, trying to rush as we wrapped the pile of Christmas presents that had covered the corner of the living room where the plastic tree had been decorated by all of us the week before. There were small and big boxes with names of many members of the extended family. It was the night before Christmas Eve, and we were preparing to celebrate *Nochebuena*.

The weekend before Christmas, I accompanied Mami to the shopping area on Third Avenue and 149th Street. It was a chilly day, and by the time we walked to the stores, my hands felt frozen, and I did not feel my feet anymore. On our way there, Mami explained to me that this year we would be celebrating Christmas the way it was done in America. Even though I was very cold, it gave me a warm feeling that we would be celebrating Christmas together in about a week.

"We are here to buy the gifts for everyone in the family," she said. "The days prior to Nochebuena, you will help me wrap all the gifts and label them," she added. She warned me not to tell anyone about their gifts. My siblings were supposed to believe that Santa

Claus had brought those gifts for them. "The older kid usually helps with the gifts," she explained. We spent hours searching for suitable gifts for every member of the family and the extended family as well. Mami said that it was important that everyone who was invited to the Nochebuena dinner receive a gift, however small it would be.

A few weeks before the Christmas holiday, our fifth-grade teacher introduced the class to a reading about Santa Claus. Some of the kids in class had never known about Santa Claus. He was not part of the celebrations at home, and I wondered if my parents would include him as part of the celebrations this year. In class, we discussed Santa's origins in the North Pole, and how he became known for distributing gifts around the world. To me, the similarities to the Three Kings was very evident. When I mentioned it to the teacher, she agreed with me. "Many cultural stories have similarities," she said.

Later, I quietly thought how funny it was that the Magi had been replaced by a fat old man who flew around in a sled pulled by reindeers. I wondered how his warm coat and boots would make him sweat if he went to warm weather places. And at that time, I figured out that would be the reason why he never went to the Dominican Republic. Mami caught me in deep thought when she had to repeat some of her instructions about where to hide the gifts once we got home and then wrap them when everyone went to bed that night.

On our way home, we took the bus and carried many bags that occupied the empty seat next to us. Mami seemed happy and almost gaiety when she went over the list of gifts she had been able to buy for everyone. When I inquired about my gift, she pulled the ponytail that was peeking out of my hat and said, "Don't be nosy."

Nochebuena was the Friday after we went shopping to help Santa Claus with gifts. The morning after shopping, my siblings woke up to a pile of bright colored gift boxes. They were chatty and cheerful for the rest of the week and spent a lot of time trying to figure out what was inside those boxes. It was fun watching them trying to guess, and I reminded them that if they opened any of the boxes, the gift would turn into coal. That was part of the discussion I had in class, weeks before, and it worked with my siblings.

One morning, as we got ready for school, my sister Ody discovered that there was a gift box with my name on it. I trembled with excitement, but I did not touch it. Deep inside, I was afraid the gift would turn into coal. After all, I was still eleven years old.

By the time the guests began to arrive for the Nochebuena feast, Mami had already prepared many dishes. She began to cook the night before when she arrived from work. She must have spent the entire night cooking since when I woke up, the apartment smelled like a restaurant. Many familiar spices pouring from the kitchen filled my stomach.

As soon as I got ready for the day, I headed to the kitchen to ask Mami about my tasks for the day. She told me a litany of things for which I was responsible for that day. She also told me that I was to supervise my siblings all day and ensure they completed their own tasks. *Ay, Disito!* I thought quietly as I walked away to begin my duties.

That was a very long day for me. When the guests began to arrive that evening, I had cleaned the bathroom, dusted every piece of furniture in the apartment, argued with my siblings so they could maintain the bedroom free of toys and other items they liked to leave laying around, helped Mami with kitchen stuff, and many more little tasks that were added to the list from earlier that morning.

Mami looked very tired when the festivities began, but she was also in a cheerful mood. She had time to clean up and looked very pretty despite her depleted energy level. I noticed her legs were swollen and tried to help her out even more than I already had done. Daddy came home early from work and was busy tending to drinks and the music. His eyes were full of happiness, and he proclaimed loudly how happy and blessed he was to have his family together this holiday. "It's a blessing from God," he said when saying grace at the dinner table that evening.

There were many extended family members present at the Nochebuena celebration that night. The neighbors from upstairs, who had four girls our age, also joined us. The adults danced and sang Christmas carols in Spanish. The kids played board games in the bedroom while waiting for midnight to open the gifts. I played checkers and Parcheesi with Margie, the older of the neighbor's girls who was also eleven.

"Feliz Navidad!" yelled the adults in the living room when midnight arrived. That was an indication for us, the kids, that it was time to open our presents. We ran to the living room and were greeted with hugs and well wishes by the adults that were left in the room. Not all the adults remained for the celebration after dinner.

I opened my gift with excitement. I was surprised to receive a real sewing machine, and at that moment, I thought that Santa Claus must be real after all. I also received a teddy bear who was identical to the one I had in the old country. I have kept that teddy bear for my entire life.

Angel received the robot he wanted and played with it incessantly for the rest of the Christmas holiday. He also kept his robot for the rest of his life. Years later, I rescued it from a storage box after he went away to the US Army and regifted it to him around the time he turned forty years old.

On Christmas morning, Mami woke us up to get ready for church. No one wanted to wake up that day, and she threatened to take the toys back and give them away to more appreciative children who were also needy. "Levántense!" she commanded. One by one, we filed into the bathroom to get ready for the 11:00 a.m. mass in Spanish. We wore the new clothes we received for Christmas and quickly ate the breakfast Mami had prepared for us before leaving for church as a family.

Every Sunday in church, my parents took turns in reading the Scriptures or presenting the gifts at the altar. They were very involved in parish matters, and many people seemed to know them. Parishioners often commented on how well-dressed and well-behaved we were, and Daddy said he was very proud of us for that. That Christmas day at church, we joined the parish celebration downstairs in the school gym. All kids received a gift, and families sat together to have a quick meal to celebrate the birth of Jesus. In the background, Christmas carols played out of a large boom box, and people joined in the singing as well.

When we left the celebration at church, snowflakes were beginning to fall. We exited the back side of the church through the doors leading to the school gymnasium. While in that gym, I noticed what a big distinction there was between the public school across the street and this parochial school where we celebrated that day. The windows were all clear of goo, and the walls were clean and well maintained.

Later that day, when I mentioned the differences in schools to Daddy, he said that someday, when I have my own children, he wished I would be able to send them to study at the best schools. That was not a possibility for him at that time since he was only a laborer and was already providing to us the best of his abilities. "Algun día llegará el progreso," he said about progressing someday, while rubbing my cheek.

WHEN ABI CAME TO NEW YORK

As time went on, our family seemed to continue to progress in the new country. Since our arrival in July 1971, every month seemed to become easier for us to adjust and obtain those things that were necessary to live a more comfortable life. By the time Abi arrived in the spring of '72, there were more items at our home that made everyday life more comfortable.

Abi was my maternal grandmother. Although her name was Ofelia, most people called her Abi. My parents said that when I was seven months old, one of the first words I uttered was Abi when I referred to my maternal grandmother. So that is how she became to be known, a name given to her by me, her first grandchild.

Abi was a tough lady. She became a widow while still pregnant with her third child and was not even thirty years old yet. She never remarried. She was not very happy and only became a sweet person as she approached her eighties and her great-grandchildren were born.

Abi used to boast that I was her favorite person because I was her first grandchild. That placed ongoing pressure on me to always live up to her expectations. She had a stern character for everyone but was mostly nice to me. Abi was the only person in my family who I know to be illiterate. She told me once that she attended school only for two years, and during the US occupation of 1916–1924, the town school was occupied and later destroyed, and only rebuilt many years later. She was not able to read and only knew how to sign her name. Abi was able to recognize numbers, and that's how she was able to conduct business to support her children when she was left a widow. She also knew fractions and understood mathematical concepts. She carried her Bible everywhere. She memorized entire passages of the holy words. She was very aware of all types of sociopolitical discourse and was able to debate very accurately using statistical examples and making interconnections to support her arguments.

During the late spring of '72, Abi came to live with us. The day of her arrival was highly anticipated by my family and specifically Mami. The days prior to her arrival, Mami reorganized our apartment to accommodate her mother. A new bed was placed in our already crowded bedroom, and we had to make room in our closet for Abi's clothes as well. Our big room became so small that there was no longer any room to play. There were five twin beds, two dressers, a wardrobe stand, and one night table, along with a desk. My brother Angel's bed ended up squished in between one of the dressers and the wardrobe stand. The corner that was his original place had been reassigned to Abi.

The day Abi was to arrive became very chaotic. My uncle Ramon arrived early to accompany my parents to the airport to pick up Abi. Hours after they left, they all returned without Abi and looked very worried. They looked like they had been crying. They placed a call to my aunt in the Dominican Republic to enquire about Abi. My aunt said that Abi had missed her original flight but was able to catch the next flight to New York City and would be arriving after midnight.

Soon after the call to my aunt, the doorbell rang, and Abi was at the door. I remember my parents and my uncle crying and praying. Somehow, Abi arrived at JFK, waited a while to be picked up, and when she realized no one was there for her, she took a cab to our home in the Bronx. My uncle Ramon had not seen his mother since he arrived in NYC over seven years earlier, so he was the happiest to see and hug his mother.

Although it had been a busy day in anticipation to Abi's arrival, we all stayed up late catching up on life while being separated. She brought each one of us a present. She seemed nicer than the last time I saw her. One amazing thing that I noticed that night, was that I had grown to be slightly taller than Abi. She pointed that out the moment she hugged me. I was eleven and was already as tall as my abuela Abi. She had very long hair that rolled down to her hips. She kept it in a bun at the back of her neck and parted her hair in the middle of her head. Her auburn hair had begun to turn gray. Abi had slanted eyes, which at times changed colors from violet to very dark brown. She was strong and hardworking.

Abi used to spend most of the night praying. She belonged to a different religion from the rest of us. Sometimes she used to take me to her Evangelical Pentecostal Church. They practiced different ways of praying than Catholics. Her church had very animated services. People clapped and chanted most of the time. People told their sinful stories in front of the entire congregation, and the pastor prayer loudly over their heads. When Abi prayed at night, she often got very animated as well. Many times, she chanted so loud that it scared me and my siblings, especially when she mentioned the devil and repentance. She often prayed for each member of the family. She named each one and added long-winded intentions and requests to God. She also followed each name with their address. I often wondered if she knew that God has knowledge of everyone's whereabouts.

According to Abi, her church did not allow their members to wear pants, nor makeup, or jewelry. They couldn't listen to mundane music, nor dance. They did not drink alcohol, nor smoke. When I questioned Abi why she smoked, she said she knew she was committing a sin by smoking, but that was the only thing she continued to do after converting to her religion. "Soy humana," she said often as if to affirm her own human qualities. Abi smoked unfiltered cigarettes for more than fifty years. Surprisingly, she lived until one hundred and four and had no ailments throughout old age.

By the time Abi arrived, I was only able to read little English and could figure out many of the words I heard if people spoke slowly and if I was given a chance to process them. The week after Abi's arrival,

I had to accompany her to the Social Security Office to process her card so she could begin to work. Mami had arranged for Abi to do some babysitting for some neighbor's child, and she would get paid via an agency. I remember walking to that office with Abi. I followed the directions Daddy wrote for me on a sheet of paper. That building was not too far away from our church. We spent all day waiting for Abi to be called, and when they did, we completed the paperwork in a few minutes. I read a book while we waited and watched how people arrived and left. Some cried. Others argued. People who worked at that place were not very nice to anyone. However, Abi was able to come out of there with what she needed.

"Are you hungry?" Abi asked before leaving that office. On our way home, Abi took me to eat pizza, and we both enjoyed a slice with pepperoni on top.

Abi continued to live with us until she was able to save money and move on her own. She was always an independent woman, and coming to the United States would not change her ways. She continued to be very active in our lives and always helped my parents with childcare issues until we were old enough to care for ourselves.

LAST DAY OF SCHOOL IN 1972

"So how was the last day of school for all of you?" asked Daddy as he sat to have dinner with us that hot and humid evening in late June. "I have seen all your report cards and noticed some certificates and medals on the living room stand," he added as he was interrupted by the sounds of firecrackers outside the back alley of our building. The rest of the dinner time conversation was filled with the same cracking noise. Daddy said it would be like this for the next few weeks in anticipation of the celebration of Independence Day on July 4th.

Our dinner table was full of delicious dishes that Mami and Abi prepared to celebrate our last day of school. "!Delicioso!" They prepared each one of our favorite dishes, and it reminded me of a Christmas Eve celebration. My siblings and I had all moved up to the next grade and received certificates of achievement for several accomplishments. We had all completed our first year of school in our new land, and our parents were beaming with pride. Before we ate that day, my parents said a prayer to thank God for all his guidance and love for our family. When it was Abi's turn to pray, I held on tight to my siblings' hands and closed my eyes to contain my laughter. Abi was known to have very long-winded and animated prayers.

There were bilingual conversations across the table. My siblings had begun to speak English by the end of our first year in school. Ody was still the most fluent. I lingered behind because I was afraid of mispronouncing words, and it made me uncomfortable when people asked me to repeat myself because they did not understand what I said. I had memorized the color chart's pronunciation in my classroom, and all the types of vowels sounds in English. Sometimes when I spoke English at length, I would close my eyes and envisioned the phonics chart to remember the various pronunciations for the vowels and different syllables.

I often discussed the complexity of vowel combinations with my classmates Martha and Rafaela, who were also learning at my pace in school. We supported each other all the time when things got difficult in English class. Most of the kids in my fifth-grade class were friendly, but few were new students to this country. The three of us had that in common, and we bonded flawlessly.

The last day of school in fifth grade was very rewarding to me. I received the most awards in my grade and returned home with a big folder full of certificates and medals. My siblings also came home with certificates. At the dinner table, Daddy spoke about the importance of doing things right and excelling at whatever the task at hand. "Doing the right thing even when no one is watching," he emphasized. "It's important to do the best work possible all the time," he proclaimed as he smiled with pride. The years ahead, Daddy preached to us about those values of honesty and hard work. That speech remained with me for the rest of my life as a student, as a professional, and as a parent.

At dinner that day, Abi also spoke about her lack of formal education and lack of opportunities back in her hometown. She told us that although she could not read nor write, she taught herself to recognize numbers so that she could do business when she became a young widow with three young children. She learned to recognize the currency so that she would not get shortchanged by vendors. She also memorized entire passages of the Bible and carried her Bible to church every time as her guide through life. That evening at the dinner table, she said how proud she was of her four grandchildren for their success during a very difficult first year in the United States. "May God bless you all, my children," said Abi as she clapped, rejoiced, prayed, and congratulated us along with our parents.

At the end of our dinner, we celebrated by eating ice cream, which was enjoyed by all. It very hot and humid that night, symbolizing the beginning of the summer in New York City. We told funny stories about Daddy's multiple jobs. We laughed about Mami's first time taking the subway on her own, Abi's arrival after midnight, and the first day of snow for the kids. We remembered our first day of school in New York. I told them about the awful cafeteria food that looked like cat food. We also recalled our first trip to the Statue of Liberty and the move at midnight. Abi laughed along with us listening to those stories for the first time.

As we told stories, we hugged each other and clapped for some of the dramatic ones told by any of us. Our time together as a family sitting at the dinner table was part of great memories my parents wanted to always create for us.

That last day of school created a good excuse for us to celebrate for hours after eating dinner. Softly, in the background, we listened to the Spanish ballads Daddy played in the stereo system. We all did short performances for our parents, versions of the ones we had performed at school throughout the year. Loli and I recreated a short version of the play we did during the November celebration. No one seemed to get tired of telling stories and laughing. Even Mami was very jolly that evening, and that time, she did not mind that we were all talking at once and laughing incessantly.

SERVICE AND COMMUNITY

My siblings and I grew up in an environment where material items were scarce and unnecessary wants were frowned upon. Papi was a simple man who carried himself with elegance and placed great importance on the individual's value for what they carried inside their heart and their head. "The feelings come from the heart," he often said. He also talked about the virtues of simplicity and hard work. Sharing what little we possessed was drilled in our way of life at home. Looking around and finding out how we could be useful was my parents' never-ending discourse.

Once, Angel came home from school to collect some of his clothes and toys. He packed them in his backpack, and when Mami questioned him about that, he said that there was a poor classmate with whom he wanted to share some of his clothes and toys. Mami took out the items out of his bag and only allowed Angel to give away one of his shirts and one toy. When she explained to Angel that we were also poor and that what little we had, we had to cherish, he began to sob because he never realized before that we were also poor. Over time, Angel would continue to give away some of his things to other kids in school who he claimed needed it more.

When my sister Loli and I became teenagers, we joined the church group Daughters of Mary. Part of the requirements entailed volunteering at the nearby elderly care facility one full Saturday a month. The first day we spent time helping nurses' aides roll wheelchairs and ensuring that the residents on the floor we were assigned were ready to attend the various activities being held that day. Some were wheeled to the theater to watch a musical comedy group. Others were wheeled or accompanied to the game room to play bingo or card games. The Daughters of Mary group of about fifteen girls spent all day transporting the elderly to various locations. Months later, that group of fifteen volunteers was down to four. My sister and I, along with two other girls, were the only ones who continued to assist for years to come.

To be honest, the volunteer work at the home was not my favorite place. I did not like the smell in that place. Every time, upon returning home, I felt the need to change my clothes and shower from head to toe to remove all traces of the smell. Mami used to say that my attitude toward this work was sinful. She used to lecture me about humility, and eventually she began to sound like the Mother Superior at the old school. She used to pray that God would forgive me for my actions. Although I did not enjoy that type of volunteer work, I continued to volunteer until I went away to college.

One of the few things I used to enjoy about working at the home for the aged was listening to stories told by several of the residents. I loved the stories told by the oldest resident at the time. It was known that she was over one hundred and ten years old at that time. She was born on the island of Puerto Rico when it was part of Spain. She said she lived through the war of 1898 when the United States took over the island. She arrived in the US mainland after WWII to work in the garment industry. That old lady was my favorite person to wheel around. She did not smell like the rest of the other residents.

Unlike me, my sister Loli enjoyed caring for the residents who were most ill. She used to come home with all kinds of stories how she helped the nurses' aide change this person's diaper and other more graphic stories. Loli went out of her way to help organize activities and volunteered an entire week when there was a nursing strike. Years later, my sister Loli studied hospital administration in college and eventually became a prominent administrator at a large philanthropy in Manhattan, where she devoted over twenty years of her life.

As a child, my sister Loli used to catch daily beatings from abuela Abi and Mami. It seemed that both adults used to take turns into finding reasons to beat my sister. Loli was an active young child who was very curious about all types of things. Loli had a strong will, and several times I watched her defy authority. Like the time she told the Mother Superior at our boarding school that she would not eat food that was meant for pigs. It turns out that one day, the meal served at our school was made from a wheat grain which resembled that which was fed to the livestock at our abuelo's farm. Although the lunch monitor nun explained to my sister that the food being served was not the same as the ones used for the pigs in a farm, my sister insisted that it looked and smelled like it.

The Mother Superior was called, and after some verbal exchange, my sister challenged her by throwing the plate of food at the nun's feet. When I saw my sister's actions of defiance, I was sure she would get killed by the Mother Superior. Amid the commotion, one of the other nuns carried my sister's little body out of the cafeteria as she kicked and screamed. I was paralyzed by the screams of desperation and pain as the nun ran down the hall and her silhouette disappeared with Loli. As I remember, my sister was not seen for the next few days, and I was sure she had been killed by the nuns. I was worried sick and wondered what would happen to my little brother and me next. At six and seven, Angel and Loli were the youngest students at the boarding school at that time.

The next day, I went to the sewing room to help Sister Juana with hemming. When I inquired about my sister's wellbeing, she told me that Loli was being punished by staying in the solitary room, but I did not believe her. I needed more evidence. Another day, I walked around the perimeter of the school and figured out where this so-called solitary room was located. Eventually, when no one was watching, I found a way to communicate with Loli by talking to her via the little window on the side of the rose garden, which led to the place that I assumed was the solitary room. The window was very high up for me, and I could not see in. Although I never saw my sister the days she was in that room, I did hear her voice whispering that she was well. To my pleasant but confused surprise, Loli claimed that she was happy to be in seclusion. I was relieved that she survived the ire of Mother Superior, the almighty Sister Mercedes. It was well known that the Mother Superior used her wide leather belt to whip anyone who defied her authority. I had seen the bruises and scars on some older students, and I was afraid that my sister had been a victim of such punishment. Loli was a very skinny little girl, and I was afraid that belt could cause great harm if it had been used on her. Those days away from my sister, I was not able to concentrate in schoolwork. I thought all the time about finding a solution for this issue. I wondered what Mami would do if she found out that her child had been harmed by anyone. It made my stomach revolt with ire to know that I was not able to do anything to help her get out of that situation. It made me even more nauseated to know that my siblings and I were stuck in this school controlled by a mean Mother Superior until my parents would send for us someday God knows when. No amount of inconspicuous and mischievousness from my part could alleviate my discomfort at knowing that we were in danger at this school. I glued one of the nun's habits to her veil. I placed a thumbtack on a desk chair. I added salt to one of their drinks. I loosened the rope on one of the clotheslines. When I heard them comment about these events, I secretly laughed inside my heart.

During one of my conversations via the little window up above the wall to the solitary room, I learned from Loli that Sister Juana, the sewing room nun, had rescued my sister from being physically harmed by the Mother Superior. When Loli was allowed to leave solitary room a few days after her defiance, she told me how Sister Juana had convinced the Mother Superior to allow her to join them at mealtime at the nuns' dining room. Loli told me that during the first meal, Sister Juana told the nuns how my sister needed much love and support since our parents had left to the US and my sister, being the youngest girl at school, was suffering from that traumatic separation. I do not remember that my sister got into much more trouble after that incident.

During the time we were both volunteers at the elderly center, my sister exhibited great qualities as a caring, loving, and selfless person. She seemed to enjoy devoting time to caring for the aged. Her attentiveness was well appreciated and evident when she walked the halls of that center and the elderly flocked toward her. Unlike me, she did not mind their smell, nor their lack of focus, nor their inability to retain information, nor their constant need of attention.

As an adult, my sister became one of the most fair-minded and even-tempered people that I know. Although she is not the elder in the family, she has taken that role by organizing family reunions and taking care of my parents' well-being as they aged. Although I am the oldest of my generation in my family, I do not have the will, patience, nor desire to lead the way as Loli does. Her keen wit is well recognized and admired. She also became the oficinista professional that Abuelo entrusted us to be when my siblings and I left our homeland.

I COULD FINALLY
SPEAK ENGLISH

I accompanied Mami in the middle of the night to Montefiore Hospital. My brother, Angel, had a bad nosebleed, and Mami was not able to control it at home. Daddy was not home yet from working late, and we had to hail a cab on the Grand Concourse. Angel was very weak since he had lost so much blood. Before leaving our home, Mami packed a few towels in a bag and wrapped Angel's head, leaving only a small opening for his breathing, in another bigger towel. "Carry this bag while I carry your brother," she said as she held him up and accommodated his head over her shoulder.

Mami had to carry him over her shoulders as we walked up the steep street leading to the big avenue. Angel's feet dangled on and interfered with every step Mami took up the street. It was a cold and windy night. Luckily, a cab stopped when we arrived at the corner, and we got into the warmth of the back seat. Mami struggled to control the bleeding as the cabdriver complained about keeping the seat clean. She used the towel that was inside the bag to change the one she had placed over his head before leaving our home.

By the time we arrived at the hospital, Angel's head towel was again all wet with blood. Following Mami's instructions, as soon as the cab pulled into the emergency room driveway, I got out and ran in to find someone who could help. I asked a nurse for help, and she met Mami halfway. The nurse led us into a small room with a stretcher, where Mami placed Angel. Other people wearing white coats entered the room to review Angel. They asked Mami all kinds of questions, which I had to translate and reply in English.

I watched how a younger man wearing a white coat sat Angel up and propped his head back while pinching the space between his nose and his eyes. Soon after, the bleeding stopped. The hospital staff asked me to tell Mami that they will need to keep Angel in the emergency room for a few hours. Mami cried as she desperately explained that my brother often got nosebleeds in the middle of the night when the weather was cold. "No es mi culpa," she also insisted that I tell them that it was not her fault or lack of care which produced such hemorrhaging on her only son. The nurse assured Mami that it was not uncommon for some children to have a nosebleed. Mami calmed down a bit after I explained to her what the nurse said, but quietly continued to shed tears all night.

As I interpreted the exchange between Mami and the people at the hospital, I surprised myself at my ability to understand almost all of what I was being told in English and was able to reply quickly. I was able to determine some difficult context from the body functions and the medical words which were like Spanish. Whenever I did not remember a word, I would motion to the part of the body or act out the symptom to allow them to understand what I meant. In my head, I had just realized that I had begun to master this new language. It had taken me over two years for that moment to happen.

While waiting to be dismissed from the emergency room, a nurse approached us and asked Mami if she would allow me to translate for a family who had arrived at the emergency room. At the time I was finishing my translation with that family, I had to assist with interpreting for an elderly man who arrived at that moment. I remember feeling nervous about translating for fear of making mistakes that could hurt people. The nurses were very nice and gave me a wrapped sour candy, which I devoured with glee.

The sun was coming out by the time we arrived home with Angel. He was able to walk on his own. Mami went on to shower and begin to get ready for her Saturday job. Since I did not have school that day, I went to bed after taking care of my brother.

The following day, when we sat down for dinner as a family, Mami told everyone how I translated the conversation at the hospital. She boasted about how I also helped other patients with their language barriers. I received a big hug from Daddy. "Estamos muy orgullosos," said Daddy. My siblings clapped as usual as when any of us received accolades.

Little did I know that I had become the official family translator. After the word got around to the cousins that I was able to translate, they often reached out to me so that I could translate documents and conversations. Eventually, Loli became a reliable translator as well, and the two of us fluidly conversed and read in either or both languages at once at church, our summer job, and our community service place.

REACHING A NEW AGE

Every summer during the month of August, Mami took all four kids for our yearly medical checkup. The satellite clinic, part of Montefiore Hospital, two blocks away from home had become our regular medical spot. Every time we came to this place, the nurses were very friendly and accommodating. They always asked about Daddy and sent their regards. They knew him from the grocery store, where they often purchased sandwiches and snacks.

During one of the visits, the main nurse in charge of pediatrics asked to speak to Mami and for me to translate what she was about to tell her. Nurse Bellamy said to tell my mother that the next time I was to visit the doctor, I would have to go down the hallway to the teenage section of the facility. I had to ask Nurse Bellamy to explain the term to me since I was not very familiar with it. I was still trying to adapt to all the different ways of life in the new country.

When I explained to Mami that I was a teenager and that the pediatrician would no longer be able to continue to see me, she began to sob. "!Ay, Dios mio, she is still a baby!" exclaimed Mami. Nurse Bellamy attempted to console her and explained, through me, that I was already growing up and needed specialized care. Mami cried even more as I tried to explain.

On the way home following Mami and my siblings leading the way, Mami admonished me about not thinking about the idea that I was all grown up already. She said that I continued to be her little girl regardless of what the medical office had said. "Don't start to think you're all grown up," she said with an attitude. Days earlier, Mami had said that I was grown up enough to take care of the home chores all by myself.

That night, when Daddy came home to have dinner with us, he inquired about our trip to the doctor. It was obvious that he already knew about Mami's tears at the doctor's office. Perhaps Nurse Bellamy had stopped by the store and told him about the incident.

My siblings were happy to inform me about their immunization shots and how they didn't cry. I hated needles and never enjoyed shots. I was also very confused about being a teenager and couldn't wait to talk to my friends Martha and Rafaela about it. They surely would know more about the subject and would be able to answer some questions that had been brewing in my head since earlier that morning.

That night, as I lay in bed thinking about my new coming of age, I wondered how was it that my mother had survived all stages of life and faced all her fears yet turned into a strong woman. Since we arrived in this country, Mami had always been overly protective of us. Her fears were evident every time she encountered a new way of thinking or a new way of doing things. Her constant way of looking at the negative side of things was getting to be exhausting, even at thirteen.

My abuela Abi was more daring than Mami. Although she was careful when walking the streets, she was not afraid of anything that came up on the way. By now, Abi lived by herself in her own apartment in a building around the corner from us. When I told her about my becoming a teenager, she hugged me and told me I was almost grown up. She shared with me that I must begin to be careful of people who would want to lure me into doing certain things.

Although she never said what those things were, I knew from conversations with friends that they had to do with relationships with the opposite sex and with adults trying to offer things that would eventually become habitual. Smoking, drinking, drug use, and hanging out in the streets were none of the things I was ever interested in practicing.

The week after my medical checkup, my friends and I finally had a chance to meet at school. We were very happy to see each other after a summer in between. When we met for lunch and recess, we chatted the entire time. Both Rafaela and I had turned thirteen that summer, and Martha was about to join in at the end of September.

We were in a new school and promised to stay together until we graduated and went off to high school in two more years. That very first day in middle school, we were so enthusiastic about our rekindling that we totally missed the obvious signs of the tough life ahead of us at that place. It was not until a few days later that we noticed that our new school environment was dangerous, chaotic, and not conducive to learning. Once we realized that, we made sure that we would protect ourselves and attempt to ignore the issues around us.

Unfortunately, by the summer we graduated middle school and were set to go onto high school, my friend Rafaela had been impregnated by one of the boys in our class. I never heard from her again since her parents sent her away somewhere. Martha moved to a different state with her mother. I went off to the high school selected by my parents to start yet a new coming of age as a high school student.

Meanwhile at the middle school, the environment became unbearable at times but helped me and some of my friends create both mental and physical barriers that protected us from many of the dangers we encountered with our new coming of age. I have some mixed memories of the time spent at Toscanini Junior High School.

I GOT MY RING BACK

By the time I attended middle school, I was already fluent in English. Somehow, I remained in the bilingual program. Some of my classes were in the honors program, so I took those classes as part of the monolingual group. My friends from elementary school had the same schedule as me. I was also enrolled in interesting classes other than academic ones. I loved the technical shop classes, although I was one of only two other girls in both the metal class and the woodshop class. The following year, when I took sewing, there were only girls in that class.

The middle school was walking distance from my home, but since I had a far walk along some isolated streets, my abuela Abi used to walk me to and from school every day. By the time I was in eighth grade, I convinced my parents that I could walk to and from school with some of my friends. That arrangement lasted only a while, and escorted walks resumed after the ring incident. Abi used to walk slow, and I often left her behind, and that became part of my argument when I presented my idea to Mami and then Daddy.

Unlike the elementary school, the middle school was dangerous both inside as well as its surroundings. There was graffiti in the hallways and the stairwells. The hallways were void of proper lighting, and the paint on the walls was mostly peeling off. There was a musty smell like the one at the first school where my siblings and I spent the first month of our first year of school.

There were students who belonged to various rival gangs and often fought over control of space both in school and outside. I learned about gangs when I asked the older cousins one day after the first week in middle school. But no one was able to explain why they insisted on fighting all the time. There were multiple fights every day in the cafeteria. There were fights in the stairwells and in the hallways. There were fights in the bathrooms. There were fights in the gymnasium and inside classrooms. Sometimes, there were multiple fights, and teachers and administrators ran all around the school trying to control the chaos. At first, I used to get very nervous about so much commotion in my middle school. Eventually, I became immune to the chaos and learned how to tune out most of the noise. Daddy taught me to pray in silence and hum to a favorite song to control my fears. I learned from others to keep alert without appearing interested in others' businesses.

After weeks of existing in that chaos, I convinced my science teacher to allow me to remain in his lab during lunchtime. I used to bring a sandwich and juice from home. In exchange, I would maintain the lab and keep it organized. My friend Martha agreed to do the same, so both of us skipped the lunch chaos most days. One day, while cleaning some test tubes, I spilled a liquid which burned through my sleeve and created a permanent mark on the side of my arm. I have that permanent mark on my forearm for the rest of my life. My teacher was very upset and nervous. He also apologized for not telling us not to touch that chemical as he usually cautioned us when he did not want something to be touched.

I remember a time when the teacher was absent for a long period of time, and we were not allowed to remain in the lab. One of those days, while returning to class from the cafeteria as we walked the several flights of steps that led to our classroom, numerous students were intercepted by members of a gang. The gangsters took everything of value we possessed. As most days, I wore my ring with the word *love* on it. Daddy gifted that ring to me when I turned thirteen to celebrate that I had reached a new stage of my life. "Don't move," said one of the boys who intercepted my friends and me as he took out a sharp knife and pointed it at us while his buddies grabbed everything they could from our necks, our fingers, and our wrists. I trembled and breathed very hard when I saw the shiny metal flaunted near our faces.

By the time we reached the fourth floor, where our classroom was, we were all crying and very agitated. The teacher sent for a school administrator, and we had to write a report of the incident. My hands were shaking so hard that I could barely hold the pen to write my experience. About a dozen students had been robbed of their valuables, and I remember one student was hurt in the process, and she was taken to the nurse's station in our school.

The ring event created a lot of anxiety in me and in my parents. Mami sighed more often than ever, and her faraway gaze seemed to get extended beyond the actual space where she was. Abi prayed more ardently than usual, and Daddy hugged me more often than before. I was not able to eat well for days.

At night, I remained awake with visions of the shiny knife waved near my face. For days after that, I used to get a knot in my stomach every time I entered the school building. Going from one classroom to the other and walking up and down the stairs produced tremors to my knees and made my hands tremble and palms sweaty. My blouse used to get wet from sweat dripping down my underarms and along my back. It made me furious that none of my friends nor I could defend ourselves from those gangsters at the time of that incident. It made me irate that they took my ring. It made me mad that my parents now had to worry about my safety inside the school.

After the ring event, Daddy got into the habit of showing up at school during recess time. He became such a familiar face, that my friends got used to call him Daddy. Somehow, he also came to know and be recognized by some of the gang boys, and they listened to him when he spoke to them. I watched Daddy from a distance as he spoke to these boys, and they seemed to listen attentively. When he approached them, they greeted him. When he left, they waved goodbye. One time later, I saw one of those boys in church, and Daddy welcomed him to the Sunday mass.

Weeks after my friends and I had been robbed, the assistant principal, Mr. Krasner, came into our science class and asked for my friend Rafaela and me. He instructed us to follow him to his office. As we walked down the gloomy hall and two flights of stairs down to his office, Rafaela and I held each other's arm in arm. We could feel each other shake with anxiety. My hands got very clammy as I walked. When we entered his office, one of the boys who had robbed us was sitting on a side chair. Upon seeing this boy, I wanted to jump at him and scratch his face but knew I could not fight a gangster.

The assistant principal instructed the boy, whose name was Adam, to speak. Adam apologized for participating in the incident about getting us robbed. He had tears in his eyes. He smelled like dirty laundry and wore wrinkled and stained clothes and had an unkept afro. His nails were long for a boy and were also dirty. Mr. Krasner then handed Rafaela her chain with her name on it and me, my ring, which had the word *love* and a very small ruby inside the letter *O*. Ruby was my birthstone, and Daddy bought it specially for me on my birthday.

I was happy to have my ring returned to me after weeks of that horrible event in the stairwell at the middle school. During recess, that boy Adam told me he knew my father from the grocery store, and that's why he had recovered my ring. He also told me not to worry about my safety any longer because he would take care of me in school. "Don't worry, your dad is a good man," he said before he walked away with his buddies. I still did not like that boy Adam.

That afternoon, I went home and wrote in my journal about getting my ring back. When Daddy came home for dinner, I shared the events of the day. He was glad that I was happy about my ring and said that he would continue to pray for my safety at the middle school. He also said that he would pray that I should eventually forgive those boys and that I stopped worrying about life issues. "Hay que perdonar," he insisted.

At the dinner table, Daddy continued to say that those boys had never had the guidance and love that I had the privilege to receive at home. He added many more things about young people's need for the proper upbringing and the lack of it he had seen in our current neighborhood since working at the bodega. He said that one of the reasons why my siblings and I were not allowed outside alone was because there was nothing good to be acquired by hanging out in the streets all the time. He emphasized that the gangster boys we saw in the streets and at school were showing behaviors natural for children who did not have proper role models and who were lacking loving care from their family. "We must pray for them because they are unfortunate children," he told us. "You must learn to forgive and forget, Angelita," Daddy said to me before he left to continue to work at the grocery store across the street.

After completing my house chores that evening, I continued to write that day's experiences in my journal. I wanted to make sense of many dangers that surrounded our neighborhood and many issues that were unresolved and unanswered by adults in charge. I wanted to know solid answers to many of my questions and continued to have concerns, not just for my safety but for the safety of the rest of the members of my family. There were many questions that I had whose answers I only learned with time and circumstances which were not explained while growing up in a very hostile environment outside the confines of our home.

A SWEATY NIGHT ON
A WINTER DAY

For a long time, I walked the four blocks from home to the middle school with a sense of being watched by some stranger. From the corner of my eyes, I learned to discern shapes and movements around me. I also got into the habit of crossing the street whenever I saw more than two boys walking or hanging together at the entrance of any building. Survival instincts kicked in when I felt in danger, and as of late, that was a common feeling. I began to distrust every stranger who passed by me. I was a fourteen-year-old skinny brown girl in a jungle of strangers, burned buildings, and garbage in the streets. I took on to wearing only pants and sneakers to school. I felt that I must always be ready to run if needed. I was a good runner in gym class and had participated at events held with other schools. I also chose not to look too attractive unless I was going to church or out with the entire family.

Getting my ring snatched by a group of gangster boys in school had only exacerbated my sense of vulnerability in this ever-dangerous environment to which my parents had brought my siblings and me three years earlier. The constant reminder of violence was ever present due to all the signs of decay around the streets of the Bronx—noise, fires, arguments, dilapidated buildings, nonworking people, addicts loitering the streets, youth hanging out instead of attending school. All these things were very visible, and I did not understand why adults who were in charge were not doing enough to fix these problems in a city that claimed to be the financial center of the world. I was barely a young teenager and could already identify these problems and had some ideas on how to address them.

Among all this chaos, my abuela Abi always waited for me at school dismissal, and she accompanied me home. Since that incident in school, I did not feel safe even when around my abuela. Abi was a strong woman for her age. She was short and stocky but was very agile and could sense danger anytime with her eagle like eyes. Although she walked behind me every afternoon since I began middle school, lately I felt uneasy when I heard commotion near me, and her presence made little to abate my anxiety. Since that incident, Daddy would drop me off at school most mornings; Abi would wait for me every afternoon.

On our walk to and from school, we encountered newly abandoned buildings more often. After every fire, the buildings were boarded up, and men of all ages would sit by the stoops to sleep or just look like zombies. I often wondered out loud why they did not go to work like the other men I knew. As we passed by them, the smell of dirt, alcohol, and burning weed would permeate the zone. Abi always prayed as we walked by. Later, at home, she would comment about every minute detail we encountered on our way. And as she related all these details, she prayed for the souls and health of those "*vagabundos,*" as she called them.

I spent many nights awake shaking and sweating when in my mind, I lived again the events of the past weeks at school. One winter night, I was suddenly woken up by screaming in the distance. At first, I did not know which direction the sounds were coming from. I hid under my blankets and held my teddy bear tight to my chest. I felt the warmth of my cat as she slept by my feet. After the screams, I heard running steps of what seemed to be high-heeled shoes accompanied by more running of two different pairs of footsteps.

The sounds went past our building and continued down the block on Sherman Avenue and down the street toward the abandoned lot down the next corner toward the building under construction. From the direction of the steps, I knew where the runners were located and where they were heading. As the steps dissipated, I heard a shot in the distance, and then, silence.

Under my blankets, in the safety of my home, I was petrified. I recognized the noise of gunshots from earlier experiences back home in the old country. As a little kid in the Dominican Republic, my family lived near a naval academy in Boca Chica. Every morning and every afternoon, the cadets would practice in the nearby shooting range. As a kid, I grew accustomed to the distant sounds from the shooting range. Later, when the US Marines took over, the sounds of shooting became real instead of practice. When I heard them at that time, I would also hide under my blanket. Adults would become very somber whenever shots were heard during the occupation of our country, and they spoke very quietly so children could not hear.

I was petrified and sweating under my blankets in that cold night because I knew someone out there in the street had gotten hurt. I did not know the story behind the screaming, nor did I want to investigate it, but I knew from the screaming, the running, the commotion preceding the shot, that the story behind was not a good one. At some point, there were sirens. Moments later, silence and more sirens that faded away.

I did not sleep the rest of the night. By the time the sun came out, total silence had finally come about. When I finally got the courage to get out from under my blankets and look out the window, snow was on the ground, and there was solitude in the street. The white coat of snow seemed to cover the chaos of the hours before. Left behind, there was no evidence of the struggle I had heard the night preceding the morning. The screaming had vanished in my ears only, not in my head. I wondered who else had heard it. I also wondered who else had followed the footsteps with their ears. I assumed someone heard the shot since the police and ambulance sirens made their presence a while after I heard the shot.

That morning, as I got ready for school, I listened attentively to the morning news. Daddy liked to listen to Radio WADO, the Spanish news station every morning. There was no mention in the news about the incident that kept me awake the night before. As we walked to school and Daddy held my hand, he asked why my hand was shaking. As we shuffled our feet through the fresh coat of light snow, I briefly told him about the gunshot story the night before. He listened and held my hand tighter than usual and then changed the subject by pointing out the sound of birds as we passed the big leafless tree near the school.

"Listen, spring will be here soon, my little Angie, beautiful flower," Daddy said with a smile when birds chirped.

As we approached the school's main entrance, Daddy blessed my forehead followed by a kiss, then he waved at a group of boys standing by the corner, greeted the school principal, and proceeded to rush off to work.

Daddy's comment about the birds had calmed my anxiety. I soon forgot about the incident I heard the night before and looked forward to listening to the birds again when I passed by that tree after school dismissal. At the time, I think Daddy's easygoing attitude toward life issues was beginning to show an impact on my way of looking at social ills.

NAVIGATING THROUGH
THE NEW AGE

I turned fifteen the summer before attending high school. That summer, I worked at the summer camp located at our local church. Sister Marie was the director, and she offered me a job to be one of her camp counselors. I enjoyed working under her supervision and made sure that I was active in all aspects of the camp activities.

Before I joined the camp as an employee, I had to convince my parents to allow me to get working papers so that I could receive pay for my work. Mami, as usual, placed resistance upon the process, and I had to ask for the assistance of my abuela Abi to convince her that this would be a good thing for me to earn my own money during the summer.

By the time I turned fifteen, I had become very aware of my mother's manipulations and exaggerations. "She's scared of her own shadow," I heard myself say aloud while I took a long hot shower one day and was thinking about my life as a teenager in my parents' home. Mami's dramatic episodes of fear about everything her children did was becoming more than annoying; it was unbearable.

When my little sister Ody was selected to attend a summer sleep-away camp organized by the NYC Archdiocese, I discussed it with Mami and attempted to convince her that this was a good opportunity for Ody to get out of the city and learn new skills. The first time Angel's Boys Scouts organized an overnight trip in the woods, I had to also convince Mami to allow him to learn how to fend for himself. Each time, I reminded her about the times she had interfered with several of my opportunities, and as guilt sank into her, she allowed my siblings to grow.

Every time Mami pointed out to me that it was my obligation to fend for my younger siblings, I reminded her that I would continue to take that job very seriously. So during our discussions about allowing them to take opportunities offered, I brought up her own words against her own arguments. During those moments, she looked at me with a look that could cut through me, if it were a solid object. Years later, while studying psychology in college, I understood that my mother often acted out of fear of the unknown. She wanted her children to achieve. However, she was always too scared of the unknown world ahead and afraid of losing them to the wide world.

Hence, as a full-grown teenager, I slowly became a defiant growing child with an ample mind of my own. Although the move to the new land had turned me into becoming quieter than I had been in the homeland, I had developed a sense of self-confidence which provided a cushion to my new, but often tentative, posture toward life at that time. I was set in my own ways and had developed well-set goals, which I refined and adjusted as time passed. I was always ready to argue my point of view in such a quiet way that few noticed that I was often advocating for a cause. I became an advocate for my siblings, for my classmates, and even for some of my teachers in school when needed.

Father O'Hara pointed out that I could, someday, sell a broken bridge to anyone by using one of my arguments. "You're very persuasive," he used to say to me often. I could read people's intentions, I explained to him once. "Then use that gift to become an advocate," he encouraged me. At the time, I did not know the extent of his charge. With time, I have learned to use that "gift" as he called it, to advocate for my students all along my decades-long career as an educator.

At fifteen, I developed ways to convince my parents to allow me to move on with many of my desires, using as an excuse the avidity to learn, to expand my wings in this new society to which they had chosen to bring and raise my siblings and me. I used the argument that they chose to bring us here. I learned early on that the person to convince about anything was my mother since she would be the one who my dad would be turning to when in doubt. Mami was the disciplinarian and guide Daddy trusted that she would make the right choice most of the time.

Unlike many of my friends, who resorted to telling lies to their parents about most of the things they did, I preferred to announce to my parents that I was planning to do things. When I spent days visiting the city museums and parks with my friends, my mother knew of my whereabouts. My excuse was always school and learning. The last day of class in high school, when my friend's mother threw a party for her right after the morning Regents exam, my mother knew that I attended that party. While my friends went there in fear of being seen by someone who would tell their parents, I danced to my full content until it was time to go home that afternoon.

So during the first summer as camp counselor, I organized various side events and activities which Sister Marie encouraged and appreciated. She allowed me to organize the talent show, the crocheting lessons, and the Spanish language lessons. The following summers, these activities became part of the program, and other counselors lead the way to organize them.

As I became an older teenager, I continued to flourish into a typical New York City teen who wore fashion jeans with bright-colored tops and high platform shoes. When I walked down the streets of Manhattan, I blended in with the rest of the locals as I moved very fast-paced along the streets, rushing, always rushing.

WHILE IN HIGH SCHOOL

During the spring semester of eighth grade, I took entrance exams at various specialized high schools in the NYC school system. I sat one Saturday for the entrance exam to the famed Bronx High School of Science. I did not make the cut. I prepared an art portfolio and presented it along with an interview at two of the art schools in Manhattan. Although I was accepted for the programs at both art schools, my parents did not allow me to attend either. Their excuse was that both schools were in dangerous neighborhoods in Manhattan. It would also mean taking the train on my own, and my parents were adamant that I was too young for such exposure.

In September of '75, I began high school at one of the neighboring schools. Although I was part of a large high school, I belonged to the honors college-bound program, and that group of students attended school at a separate building from the rest of the other students. During the first month of high school, my parents paid one of the older cousins who owned a yellow cab to drop me off and pick me up at school. The school I attended was in a very dangerous neighborhood. It was known that the streets around it were not safe, especially for young ladies. By the end of September, I had made several friends, and we protected each other when we walked to and from school to catch the bus.

The first day I arrived in high school, I realized that my schedule still had some bilingual classes. For the rest of that day, I spent the time thinking about how to resolve the issue. Four years prior, when I was first registered in school here in the new country, I was placed in the wrong grade at that time. I promised myself then not to allow anyone else to ever tamper with my school goals and my advancement.

The second day in high school, I went to see my counselor and argued that my schedule be corrected. My arguments became demands, but my counselor ignored any sensible conversations with me. Since she was not about to listen, the following day I spoke to the assistant principal and presented my case to him. By the end of the week, my schedule had been changed to all monolingual English classes. I was part of the honors program, which is where I had been told I was heading to while still in eighth grade.

I befriended three girls who became my good friends for the time we were in high school. Noemi became my best friend for life. She was bright and enjoyed socializing. I knew her from church, and she lived not far from me. In the fall of '75, Noemi asked me to be part of her sweet sixteen celebration. I was one of the sixteen girls who participated in her fancy party. We wore matching light blue gowns and a wrist corsage. Years later, I became the godmother for her firstborn son, Robert Jr.

Narcy became another one of my friends in high school. She was wise and honest all the time. She arrived with her parents from Ecuador the same year I arrived. She always knew that she wanted to study finance. After high school, she attended a competitive private college in the Bronx since her strict parents opposed her going away. Narcy was not allowed to stay after school nor participate in any of the activities the rest of our group enjoyed. I was the only friend who her parents allowed to visit their home. She was also allowed to visit my home, and over time we became very close friends. "We are a good team of dancing nerds," Narcy would tell me when she was allowed to go dancing with my siblings and me at church dances. Years later, she was the maid of honor at my wedding.

Jackie and I were always together in school since the tenth grade. People always referred of us as the nerds who helped in the science lab. We both loved to read and discuss and exchange ideas. Together we participated in a special program at nearby Einstein College and learned how to use their biomedical lab equipment. In eleventh grade, Jackie and I entered the NYC science fair and won third place in the competition. We studied the life span of red blood cells when exposed to various elements. We both learned how to conduct research from the coach at our internship lab at the college. Jackie was very meticulous about presenting her ideas, and I often went along with her suggestions for improving our work. We got excited when we discovered new ideas and ways to modify our lab work. Our names were listed in the *New York Times* when the article was published about the competition. At that time, we beamed with pride, and we were congratulated by our lab teacher in school. On our way home, we discussed the possibilities of attending college to study science. "Imagine if we someday made a real discovery," she said more than once. Jackie earned second place in the graduating class, and I took third place. We both attended Wellesley College in the fall of '79.

Jackie and Narcy were the high school friends with whom I often discussed issues about school. We all came from households where we would be the first person planning to attend college. "Look what I found in the library," Jackie would share one day. "This is what my older cousin told me about college," Narcy came up with another time. I often shared with them what I found out from my friends who were upper classmates about issues pertaining to the college process.

Because my parents did not yet speak English fluently and had no knowledge of the school system in NYC, I learned early on to fend for myself and discover all the opportunities available for students like me. I listened attentively to upper classmates to learn about the process to follow ahead. I visited the library often and asked questions about progressing in high school. So by the time I moved out of tenth grade, I was a bit familiar with the college process. My three high school friends and I taught each other about the college process. The summer after tenth grade, Jackie and I visited our first colleges with an organization called Aspira.

Eleventh grade was very challenging for me. I took advanced chemistry, and the teacher was not an instructor I would recommend. "Open the book to page…" was his only style of teaching. "Complete activities so and so…" was his explanation. The top students in the class were all girls, and we would meet after school and teach each other by using library resources so that we could pass the exams our teacher gave us each Friday. We memorized the entire periodic table of elements and became very good at guessing what would be included on the next exam.

In addition to his lack of interest in our knowledge of chemistry, our teacher smelled so horrible that my friends and I bought him a cologne set for Christmas. As it turned out, he did not accept the gift and got very offended because he was not a Christian. I remember thinking that he should have just taken the gift and explained to us nicely that his religion did not practice our beliefs. After all, our English teacher was not Christian, and he welcomed our gifts and cards every year. By the end of the term, many of us did not achieve the level of mastery we would have preferred in chemistry. My friends and I were unhappy. We discussed how that may have impacted our overall average and our state exam scores.

Not all my high school teachers were a waste of time. Throughout the years since high school, I have credited my global history teacher, Mr. Reynolds, for instilling in me a sense of civic duty to global issues. He was my history teacher for two years in high school. He taught with enthusiasm and welcomed comments and new ideas. He was a good listener and one of the few teachers who encouraged all students to achieve.

When my friends and I complained about our guidance counselor, Mr. Reynolds would tell us to find help in other sources. He introduced us to various agencies that would help first-generation university students with the college process. When Jackie and I received acceptances and scholarships to all the colleges we applied to, it was Mr. Reynolds who suggested that we make a list of all the pros and cons about each school before deciding where to attend. When I became an educator years later, I followed Mr. Reynold's example to inspire my students to reach for the best of their abilities and encouraged them to thrive no matter what the circumstances.

The honors program was transferred to the main building in the middle of tenth grade, and my friends and I were very upset. The week before leaving for Christmas break, we were informed during an assembly that we were to report to the main building after the break. We were going to join the rest of the high school students at the main building. We discovered that the main building housed over four thousand students. My friends and I discussed how our entire high school lives were transformed, and there were few adults in our school who cared to hear our voices.

Our counselor continued to be useless to us. Because of the permanent frown on her face, we often joked that she was constipated. She walked around with a stiff lip and was void of any smile. I never saw her laugh even when it was appropriate to do so. Like the counselor, several of the teachers did not engage in any conversation with us outside of class discussion.

Some of our classmates were transferred to other schools because their parents were afraid for their safety at the main building. Noemi was one of the students who left for another school. She transferred to where her brothers attended. She was able to graduate a year earlier because of the number of credits she had already earned in our program.

One of the few adults who listened to us as we discussed our drastic change to the main building was Mr. Valerio. He was a young English honors teacher who was very active in school. One rainy day when Jackie and I waited for the bus at the 161st Street stop by the Grand Concourse, Mr. Valerio stopped and offered us a ride to school in his car. We both hopped in the back seat, and as we rode to school, he offered to take us every time he would see us at the stop. The morning rides to school became our time to vent about various issues happening in our school building. Mr. Valerio also shared with us his disappointment for the lack of appropriate reading materials his department had received. He was another adult who would listen to our concerns.

It was the late seventies, and there were many problems at our large high school. There was rampant violence both inside the school as well as out in the neighborhood. There were overcrowded class-rooms, and as we walked the hallways during change of class, we often heard kids in regular classes complaining that there were no seats for them when the entire class attended. It was also known that many students never graduated. Other students ended up in jail or were lost to a life of violence in the streets. Listening to the tone employed by some teachers having conversations about the types of students they had to teach made me very worried about the state of our school.

"I heard the gym teachers chatting about the kids who got arrested the other day," I told Jackie as we walked to the bus that afternoon. She interjected by adding that in her art class, the teacher was having a conversation with another adult about the new Latino gang that was growing in numbers at the school. We continued to chat about the evident violence surrounding us as we walked past the new burnt building across the street. The fresh smell of smoke was still seeping through the cracks of the destroyed windows that was consumed by a fire.

The ever-present signs of poverty and violence were part of our lives throughout high school. The cafeteria was unsafe for students and adults, and the food looked very unhealthy. Most of the time, I brought lunch to school because even the sandwiches from the caf-eteria looked and tasted awful. Jackie and I befriended one of the cafeteria ladies, and she would secure for us an extra fresh fruit and a juice box, instead of the regular meal, when we purchased lunch for a quarter. I never qualified for free lunch or transportation in school since both my parents worked. Eventually, Jackie and I stopped going to the cafeteria altogether and instead spent that time in the biology lab caring for many plants in that room and helping the lab techni-cian prepare for the lab classes. It was reminiscent of middle school, when I chose to remain in the science lab during lunchtime to escape violence in the cafeteria.

Our lab teacher was an adorable lady. She looked older than my abuela Abi but was very energetic and always moved very fast to prepare for the next lab. Her cheeks were always very pink and got rosier whenever the administrator visited the lab. "These young ladies are my assistants," she would say to them. She encouraged and guided Jackie and me to participate in the city science fair. She was the only adult to accompany us to the competition and later came when we received our awards.

In junior year, she also arranged for us to volunteer at an elaborate lab at Einstein College. During our senior year, she secured a place for us to take chemistry at nearby Lehman College. Our lab teacher was the nicest person I knew all throughout high school. When I left for college, I wrote to her and let her know about my progress. She was the only person who I told about my discontent about being a premed student. She replied to the first couple of letters, but never answered any more letters after that. Someone told me later on that she had to leave work due to illness and did not return after that.

While in senior year in high school, I helped organize a student sit-in-the-hall to protest American companies' involvement in Apartheid in South Africa. Our dear global history teacher was involved in guiding his students to study a social ill and to act upon to create change. When Jackie and I heard about it, we approached him and helped the younger students organize the sit-in. Over time, I have participated in similar events to voice social discontent about issues that impact disenfranchised people both locally and abroad.

Although our high school was a dangerous place to be, my friends and I formed a bond which protected us from harm. We were intentional about our safety, our achievement, and our growth as teenagers. We did not go anywhere alone, nor walk the streets without each other. There were stairwells in our school that we knew not to transit and corners of the school where we would not go either. "Never walk alone," we told each other. The gym locker room was a known place of danger, and there were stories about things that happened to other kids. My friends and I wore our gym clothes under our regular-day outfits so we did not have to use the locker room on gym days. "We have to outsmart the thugs in this place," one of our friends would often say with a big beautiful smile filled with ivory teeth against her ebony skin. That is how I remember this girl whose name has escaped my mind over the years. "Outsmart the thugs," I would reply.

My friends and I all had overprotective parents. When Jackie and I were taking art, we convinced our parents to allow us to visit museums in Manhattan after school or during school recess days. The art teacher had encouraged us to make those visits. We would take the D Train from Yankee Stadium to Columbus Circle and walk downtown to Penn Station or up toward Fifth Avenue or Central Park West to the museums. Sometimes we walked across Central Park to the East Side or downtown toward Soho. At first, the crowds would interfere with our views and the pace of our walks. Soon we learned to walk and look around as fast as the crowd.

When Jackie and I spoke about the museum, we often meant it as the entire island of Manhattan. To Jackie and me, the island was a massive museum. During the last two years in high school, we spent many hours visiting and learning about the cultural wonders of the city. We memorized the map of Manhattan by studying the subway map. We became fascinated by the myriad of sights and opportunities offered on that island. A few years prior, we had both come from a much different island in the Caribbean. To some, this concrete and metal island, crowded with many people who looked very different from each other, was many different things. We watched some who were heading to work, others, heading home, while some were just there shopping. There were noticeable tourists, while there were locals who did not admire anything that passed by their sight. And while we studied people passing by as we walked, we sometimes noticed those who walked the city for some sinister reason like the ones who went around scouting distracted people to rob or illicit merchandise or services. Unfortunately, there were times we witnessed some of those evil acts.

We researched the places and times that allowed students to visit for free, and we took advantage of visiting those places on our days off from school. It was a great feeling to see up close some of the artwork we were studying in art class. While visiting Manhattan, we learned to also admire the architecture of some of the buildings. There were details in the older buildings that could be studied if we were staring up and carefully noticing intricate details. So several times, we just leaned against a corner light post, stared right up, and discovered the details on specific buildings.

One of my favorite buildings to look at was triangled-shaped and located around West 69 Street. The sides were embedded with many details that resembled the ornaments on the frosting of a cake. We always wanted to see the Chrysler Building up close but were never able to see it other than from below or at a far distance. As we walked the city streets, we imagined and wondered how awesome it would be to study that building from a window across the street.

Visiting Grand Central Station for the first time as a student of art was an exhilarating experience. I remember the massive amount of people rushing about that afternoon. Meanwhile, Jackie and I walked slowly in awe and stared at the magnificent windows, the arches, the design of the place, and the big ornate clock. I remember the sunlight reflecting through four of the windows and making it seem like spotlights on a Broadway show. The long dome painted like the sky seemed like an opening to the heavens above. I noticed it did need some cleaning. We both walked around for a while and excitedly shouted to each other and pointed to all the details we were able to identify as we reviewed this magnificent place. "Check that out!" I often heard Jackie say with excitement. On that tour, we heard from a tourist that sometimes the sunshine coming in from each window would converge in one spot illuminating the entire station main concourse. We were never lucky to witness that sight.

On our way home after our excursion to Grand Central Station, we discussed the beautiful details that were part of this train station and planned to return later that year to continue to discover its magic. Both Jackie and I enjoyed our expeditions of the city and tried to blend in with the crowds as much as we were able to do so. On days we visited midtown, we mimicked the dressing styles of mannequins we admired in the big stores. Sometimes, Jackie was able to fluff her hair to imitate a long downward afro with her beautiful shoulder-length curly hair. I used to decorate my bell-bottom jeans with patches to resemble those expensive jeans at the stores.

Since Jackie and I both enjoyed sewing, we also visited the fashion district a few times during our excursions. We visited fabric stores and other stores devoted to accessories only. There was a big store with just buttons located near Macy's, and that was a favorite place for me. I was amazed by the amount and variety of buttons housed in one spot. "Imagine being able to buy some of those accessories for our outfits," both Jackie and I wondered out loud. "Or imagine if we were able to purchase anything at those specialty stores and the wonderful outfits we would create," we both agreed. Usually, our train ride home after visiting the garment district was filled with those animated conversations about our creative impulses to someday produce a wonderful-fitting outfit like the ones created by the great designers.

*****

While in high school, I also discovered a taste for live performances. As part of the honors program, my classmates and I attended many Broadway plays with our English ninth and tenth grade teacher. *Hello, Dolly* was the first show our class went to see. One of my favorite musicals was *Fidler on the Roof.* The bright lights illuminating Broadway theaters was an experience all on its own. The various outfits worn by the characters was another thing I admired.

People of all kinds walked enthusiastically chatting about the facades on the theaters or the shows they had just seen or about to see. There was always a fee involved in these trips, and not always all my friends could attend. My parents always found the money for me to participate in all kinds of school events. Years later, I learned that many times, they had to work overtime or not buy their own necessities to be able to save enough money to provide my siblings and me with those enrichment opportunities. Daddy always said that his children would be provided with the opportunities available whenever possible, so that we could learn about the richness of the world surrounding us. He always said that living in the South Bronx was a necessity and a temporary period of our lives as we transitioned through the American Dream.

My English teacher in ninth and tenth grade was an older lady who wore blouses that were too long for her arms. Her heavy perfume made me sneeze often. She spoke very properly and softly, and some kids fell asleep. Since I enjoyed literature, I often asked and answered many questions. One day, when she was standing in front of the class telling us a story to explain Hamlet, she laughed so hard that part of her lower teeth fell off. Since I sat on the first row, the mouthpiece landed on my desk in between my folded hands, and I did not know what to do. I had seen that happen to my abuela Abi before, but this time, my teacher was in front of the class when this happened. All the kids laughed, and I felt sorry for her although I was stunned with the incident and probably would have laughed as well if I had not experienced those teeth fall in between my arms. When I wrote in my journal about this incident, I recall feeling very sorry and embarrassed for my teacher.

Although high school time seemed never ending, when graduation day arrived, I was somewhat sad to know that I would not be able to see some of my classmates again. Together, my buddies and I had overcome many hurdles of growing up as teenagers in this large city called New York. Most of us lived in rough areas of the Bronx, where there were distractions of all types. I knew that several of my friends were not as blessed as I was to live in a loving home with responsible parents. My own parents had to rescue some of them in prior years when their home lives became unbearable and unsafe. There were times when kids were allowed to stay with our family for days until their parents resolved whatever issues. For the senior award ceremony, my parents had to accompany one of my friends because her parents were not willing to be there for her during the ceremony.

When Mami and I went to purchase my graduation dress, we invited Jackie, and Mami bought her a dress as well. Many times, Mami paid for one of my friends' trip fees so that they, too, could have the opportunity to learn. Every time she had a chance, Mami would say that all children should be given the chance to succeed. "Every child needs to grow and be nurtured," she would often say.

I did not understand her complex personality until many years later when she began to share the hardships she encountered growing up.

When I was about to complete high school, I was happy to be able to say that I got through such a hostile environment. The streets around the high school were rough and dangerous. Not all my initial classmates from ninth grade had survived the ordeals that were encountered at our high school. The heavy toll imparted by our inner-city hostility, the pains of growing up, and the lack of support and demands imposed by some of their families had forced some of my classmates to deviate from our tightly knit honors program. Every year, some never returned to school.

As I ended this stage of my life and approached adulthood, I was happy about and thankful for many things. I was fortunate to have made good friends. I was elated to graduate with honors. I was grateful for the opportunities I was given in high school. I was satisfied that my parents were still supportive even when I had become rebellious with my constant developing thoughts and evolving personality. I was overjoyed that my siblings still liked me, despite my arrogance at times. I was most optimistic to soon be moving away to the college of my choice.

NERD WHO COULD DANCE

"**D**id any of you join the spelling bee at the district level?" asked the English teacher. It was indeed challenging for me and my classmates to belong to the college-bound honors program in high school. Each of us dealt with all sorts of obstacles. Yet these obstacles seemingly did not face us, nor were they acknowledged by the adults in our lives. The English teacher did not provide any guidance for this new contest she was inquiring about, nor were we encouraged further than just her utterance as she crumpled her face. "Ugh! You're all late to submit your registration for this competition!" At which, we just rolled our eyes as if to reply, "You could've informed us earlier."

There were merely forty students in the honors category for my graduating class. During the first two years of high school, kids in the honors class did not attend school at the main big building, where more than four thousand students were crammed into overcrowded classrooms. The honors program was housed in a separate small building located not too far from the main high school. Approximately two hundred students attended the program as well as the bilingual kids. This unique small setting was very similar in size and culture to my bilingual elementary school. There, everybody knew each other. There we had no disciplinary problems with the students, and most teachers were nice and attentive.

Upon reaching the tenth grade, at midyear, all the honor students were transferred to the main big building. Unfortunately, that became a big nightmare for many of us. Morris High School's main building was in an even more dangerous neighborhood. Its surrounding streets were filled with debris, burned buildings, empty lots, and homeless addicts who often followed students to ask them for money and food.

My friend Jackie, others in the honors program, and I walked together to the crosstown bus stop on our way home to avoid changing buses and riding the bus. We avoided the ride on the bus which stopped at the corner of the school. On nice days, we walked more than three miles home. There were stories about students getting robbed and girls getting groped on that bus route. "Have you seen how many passengers ride in that bus?" said my friend Narcy on our first day at the main building. "Let's skip the ride," motioned Jackie. That's when we decided to walk to the crosstown bus stop. That bus was also overcrowded, and kids shoved each other as they attempted to get on it all at once. So we waited for a couple of buses to go by before we got on.

The seven-block walk to the crosstown bus stop was always eventful. "Let's cross now," and we all ran across the street to avoid a drunk man who was heading toward us. "Cover your nose," I would warn as I got a whiff of putrid air spewing from an abandoned building.

My friends and I used to pass near the Fort Apache Precinct, which was amid a very stressed scene of endless vandalized buildings. The burned-down buildings near the school were surrounded by rubble of bricks, bent metal, and broken glass. "Hop!" and we all did to avoid cutting ourselves as we walked on broken glass spread across the sidewalk.

Some of the buildings were boarded up, and lots of graffiti defaced the walls that were still erect. Strangely enough, sometimes, within a pile of rubble, a young and delicate tree would perch up toward the heavens.

As we walked home, we told each other secrets and whispered the names of the boys we liked at the time. We soon discovered that the names of these boys changed often and were also cognizant that we exchanged these names as if they were just objects of a moment's desire.

Narcy was the only one who remained constant about the boy she liked. "You still like the same guy?" I asked after the long summer of sophomore year. She smiled and shrugged her shoulders as we crossed the street one more time.

We maneuvered the streets constantly and fended off all types of disturbances. We developed code words to advert each other of dangerous predators. "Bounce!" became a warning word for us, and we'd cross the street often.

As we zigzagged the streets, we learned how to outsmart many of the delinquents. There were people looking for customers to sell their drugs. There were some who were asking for change to add to their funds to support their vice. We also identified men who were in search of having a good time with young girls. Also loitering the streets were people trying to pick fights with total strangers. At times, there were also people who were trying to preach their religious ways by claiming that they were saved because they repented from their many sins. We were just a group of young girls who were simply trying to get home from school after a long day.

The cool air from the fall arrived, and soon the chill from winter began to smack our cheeks as we walked every day after school. Since daylight was scarce during the wintertime, when we left school, we were extra careful walking the rough streets at dusk in the South Bronx. We always made sure that there were at least three of us walking together.

All my senses were at full gear when I walked with my friends. With time, I learned how to use my peripheral vision to new levels. I mastered not having to turn my head to see who was approaching from behind or the sides. My keen sense of smell also helped me identify some of the dangers we faced. I learned to identify various smells on people who passed by my side on the streets. "You're like a hound dog," my friends used to say when I cautioned them about an approaching smell.

Walking the streets around the high school main building became more dangerous as time passed. It seemed that every month, a new building was abandoned due to destruction by fire. So many times, as I sat in my classroom, the smell of burning rubble would invade the air and often made me cough. Sirens were often heard in the distance, and at times, faint smoke permeated the air in the school hallways. "Which building burned down this time?" we mumbled among each other.

I often wondered where the people who were affected by those fires went to live when they lost their homes. "Where do the people go?" we questioned each other. At times, that subject became the source of our conversations as my friends and I walked to the cross-town bus stop. We made conjectures about the lives of the people who lived in those buildings. Occasionally, we read about their sad fate in the city newspapers. We also heard about some of their stories from the kids at school. Sometimes, there was even a collection of money and clothes in school to assist the arson survivors who were family members of a classmate.

"See that weird thing?" Jackie said one day, pointing to a pile of unrecognizable objects and debris on the side of the abandoned building we were passing by a that time. Beside the pile of ripped bags, dirty rags, and broken glass, there were used needles and evidence of burned objects. At the time, neither of us knew that such weird thing was remnants of the paraphernalia used by the addicts who loitered the street near our high school. As we continued to walk home, we discussed the new discovery and wondered what and why. We both agreed that some people had hard lives.

*****

My group of friends shared similar goals, and we did not allow all the distractions around us to diffuse any of our aspirations to move on to college and lead professional adult lives. None of our parents had completed higher education. Most of our parents worked long hours as laborers in factories or as homecare assistants. My dad always held multiple jobs as a laborer. Many of my friends' dads also held multiple jobs. Our parents did not understand the college process, and we knew that they were limited in the type of support they could offer. So as we approached this new milestone, preparing to move on to college, we rejoiced among each other and were happy to make our parents proud. At least those who cared about our accomplishments.

"Check out my latest letter of admission!" said Jackie as we met at the bus stop to school. That morning, she was beaming with happiness, and her eyes were brighter than usual. She showed me the letter of admission to Yale University, and I gave her a high five as I smiled. For a long time, that had been her first choice, and she had to convince her parents to allow her to attend there.

Several of us in the honors group received awards for various academic competitions throughout New York City, and we considered ourselves lucky for our accomplishments. In the spring of senior year, when the time came for us to select a college, we believed with confidence and despite all odds, that we all would become accomplished and productive adults.

I was known to be very competitive among my peers. Winning was very important to me. If I decided to spend my time on any given task, I needed to feel some type of gratification or reward. I learned early in life to be my strongest critic and often worked very hard to accomplish my set goals no matter how small or big these were. "Always forward. Look ahead," I often told myself.

I wore glasses, and most days I had two long ponytails. I dressed in simple but neat freshly pressed clothes. I often changed the styles of the outfits I bought since I used my sewing skills to customize them. I received nice compliments from my friends for my outfits. Although I seldom wore makeup, I always had neatly painted long nails and wore pink lip gloss.

I read a lot and memorized long pieces of poetry both in Spanish and English. My dad and I enjoyed reciting poetry together, and Pablo Neruda along with Ruben Dario were our favorite poets. I later introduced him to the works of Edgar Allan Poe and Walt Whitman's "Song of Myself."

Many times, I stayed after school to participate in academic enrichment programs. New business machines and telescopes had been brought to our school. My friends and I enjoyed participating in various science projects. We also took up some classes that did not fit our day schedule. We heard that typing would be necessary in college. And during my junior year, my dad bought me my first typewriter for Christmas.

*****

I had many different friends, and I enjoyed tutoring the students in the bilingual program when they needed help. When I heard that one of the main dancers in the school talent show for my junior year suffered an injury, I quickly volunteered to take her place so that her partner would not miss his opportunity to perform. The dance was a combination of salsa and disco steps. It only entailed one lift, and I enjoyed it. Those were my two favorite dances. I was a kid from the Bronx who knew about seventies' music and dance moves.

When I volunteered to help my friend, there were several students who mocked the idea of a nerd dancing to popular music. "A dancing scientist," I overheard one girl mumble as I got ready to dance during rehearsal. I quickly gave her a side-eye and dismissed her comment as ugly noise.

Only my closest friends knew I could dance to various types of music of that time. I did not socialize much at school, but kept friends of various ideologies. It was interesting to me to listen to the kids who preferred to follow technical profession paths. They looked forward to becoming secretaries, plumbers, or firefighters.

After a few hours of practice after school, and several more hours of dancing with the broom at home, I had mastered the moves, and I helped my friend earn fourth place in the talent show. I danced with my partner in front of a crowded school auditorium. "No tengas miedo," he said as he held my hand to calm my nerves before we began to dance.

When I danced, I tuned out the cheers and noise from loud teenagers. Once the performance was over, I was able to feel my knees again as they shook. I also felt like my stomach was full of butterflies. For the rest of the school year, I was known by some as the nerd who could dance.

Dancing was in my blood. I danced at home with my family all the time. Every home celebration included dancing. Merengue was the customary dance for the older generation. However, salsa and disco were the preferred dances of the young members of the family and friends.

Back in the old country, my abuelo taught me how to dance when I was very young. Abuelo used to say that music was in our blood and that we just needed to allow our feet to feel the rhythm. So this is how at the only dance competition I ever participated, I followed Abuelo's old advice. And although my abuelo was not there to see me at the talent show, I knew I made him proud that time.

AND JUST LIKE THAT, THE LIGHTS WENT OUT

One of the amazing things about living in New York City was the amount of artificial lighting there was everywhere. The streets were brightly lit all the time. The elementary school did not have any windows, but the lights were bright and shiny all day. The first day we arrived in this city, I admired in awe how each building in the distance was illuminated and bright. Dusk had begun to fall over the city, and the bright lights of the rows of buildings, traffic, and streetlights made competition with the darkness that began to cover the city.

Back in the old country, there were constant blackouts. Sometimes, the lights were off for many hours. People were used to the blackouts, and it was a natural occurrence for events to be modified all the time. There were traffic agents at the large intersections in the capital city. They controlled the traffic when electricity failed.

When we were younger, my siblings and I used to play traffic agents in our room. *Brooom, peep, peep!* We rolled our bodies across the floor and around the corners and aisles formed by our twin beds. Sometimes we used Angel's play cars and toy soldiers to police the imaginary traffic we created. We played lots of make-believe games inside the four walls of our apartment.

While in New York, there were never any blackouts until the summer of 1977. I remember just like that, as we watched TV one evening sometime in mid-July, the lights went out in NYC. That was a fun experience for me in the city. At first, there was a deafening silence across the neighborhood. No radio wars of salsa and pop music to be heard in the distance. No television programs blasting in the air.

Although the night of the blackout was hot and humid, there was a nice breeze that cooled the air at times. All the windows were open, and, in the distance, I heard various types of celebrations going on all night. There was the sound of congas in the distance. Someone played the trumpet to the sound of the popular salsa song "El Cantante." Occasionally, there were cheers, and I assumed that there were men playing table games somewhere.

The next morning, there was a lot of activity in the street. Since early morning, the water hydrant was open to the sprinkles, and kids of all ages spent the day running through it. The street was closed to traffic, and many of the neighbors brought out folding chairs and tables and shared their food and drinks with each other. Several of the older men played games of dominoes and cards for hours. Some people brought out their battery-operated boom boxes and played music. Some of the youth danced to disco music in the middle of the street.

Several times throughout the two-day blackout, I recognized the familiar smell of burning buildings in the distance. There were rumors of young people looting nearby stores. Daddy's grocery store did not suffer any violence since he closed as soon as it all got dark, and the next day he remained open only during the daytime.

At first, my siblings and I were not allowed to step outside of our apartment. We were forced to watch all the commotion and street festivities from our apartment. Mami was very adamant that the street was not safe and that "no one in their right mind would be outside today," she repeated every time we asked to go join our friends outside. We insisted so much that Mami and a neighbor decided to take us outside for a little while. They brought out folding chairs and sat by the side of the building where other ladies were sitting watching their little kids. Although we were all young teenagers, Mami continued to oversee every move we made, and the day of the blackout was not an exception.

Later, I wrote in my journal how odd I felt to walk the street up and down without a real purpose. For the first time, I met many of the kids who lived on our block. I talked to them about music and dancing. My sister Loli and I danced to disco music with some of the kids from our block. "Let's go dance," she encouraged me. And as we began to swing around, two young guys from the neighborhood broke into our dance, and we continued to dance with them. After the disco song, we moved right into a salsa dance. Dancing in the middle of the street felt weird but fun.

When we went back inside, since it was a sunny long day, I spent most of my time by a window reading and sketching in my drawing pad. During breaks from reading and sketching, out the window I observed people intermingle with each other that afternoon. I watched entire families continuously playing together in the closed street. I saw the exchange of food among people of various cultures. There was a wide display of colors in the street that day. Everyone wore bright summer colors, and people's skin colors were also all hues.

Sometime that night, there was a big cheer and roar in the air. My ears were assaulted with loud noise of music, and lights flickered a bit before going on completely. It reminded me of the blackouts in the old country and how people always cheered when the lights returned.

When the news stations reported about the blackout, I paid close attention to the events being reported. There had been a massive failure in the electric grid that affected most of the city. The news said that only parts of Queens was spared the blackout. The news also reported looting, crime, subway evacuations, and arson that consumed entire city blocks. That explained the smell of burning metal and wood in the distance I sensed before.

Later, when Mami heard the news, she pointed out her hesitancy about allowing us to be in the street that day. She compared this blackout to the ones in the home country, where they were a natural occurrence, and no one seemed to take advantage of being in the dark to harm other people nor property. Mami often used every opportunity she got to support her overzealous behavior toward our upbringing.

THE LETTERS HOME

One of my favorite things to do during my formative first years in the new country was to write letters to my abuelo, my aunts, and cousins who all remained back in the homeland. Every month, I would write letters to inform them of my progress as I grew up in the United States. Then I would eagerly wait for a reply and their questions about my well-being and that of the rest of my family members.

Writing letters to family members was the only way of communicating with them back in the seventies. They had no phone back then. There was no such thing as technology the way we came to know it in the new century in later years. My letters were elaborate with many details about everyday events in our family life here in New York. I would become creative with my handwriting and practice new styles as time passed. I learned how to write calligraphy in one of my art classes, and I used it often specially when writing to Aunt Isabel.

My aunt Isabel wrote the most loving letters. Tía Isabel, as we called her in Spanish, was Daddy's favorite sister and my favorite aunt. Every time we visited Abuelo's farm, she ensured my siblings and me were happy and comfortable. She also took care of my younger sister

Ody when my parents left us behind in the Dominican Republic. She was very artistic and knew how to sew and cook very well. Whenever I visited her house, she would let me use her sewing machine. I barely used to be able to reach the pedal to her old Singer machine, but she always found a way to accommodate it to my reach. She taught me how to use her machine, which was slightly different from that of Sister Juana's, and trusted that I would not jam it or break the needle. She instructed me how to place my hands so as not to sew over my little fingers. Tia Isabel was taller than Daddy, so she must have been tall. She always smiled and was very soft spoken and almost as loving as Daddy.

I learned how to sew from Sister Juana, the nun in charge of sewing the students' uniforms and the nuns' habits. She taught me how to use the sewing machine and fix some minor problems when it got stuck. Sister Juana taught me how to use the sewing machine since I often helped her with hemming and crafting buttonholes. Mami taught me how to hem and do fine embroidery from the time I was very young. During days off from school, I used to spend many hours helping Sister Juana in the sewing room. "Stay focused and be patient," Sister Juana said each time I huffed and puffed when completing a sewing project. She used to say that sewing was an art of love and that it was one of the oldest jobs to mankind.

When I wrote letters to my tía Isabel, I would tell her about my hobbies and my new projects. She was very excited to learn that I received my first real sewing machine from Santa Claus on the first Christmas in New York. She would often ask about the details for several of my creations, and I would reply with the outcome for each one. She would also comment on the progress of my handwriting and encouraged me to continue to experiment with learning new styles, not just with my writing but with my thought process. Tia Isabel kept me informed of my grandparents' health, and when my abuela passed away in 1972, I remember that she wrote a letter to me about how much the two of us would miss Abuela's knowledge of herbs and healthy living.

When I wrote to my tía Isabel about taking woodshop in seventh grade, she wrote back about how she would have loved to learn such skill. "Me encanta esa idea," she wrote. I told her that I was only one of two girls in that class and that my classmates were all very protective of the two female students, and the teacher did not allow us to use the heavy electric saw for fear that we would get injured. She wrote back encouraging me to speak to my teacher about showing me and allowing me to use that machine. In her letter, she told me to let my shop teacher know that the saw was not much different from a sewing machine. At the end of the school semester, I earned an award for building a neat birdhouse with very good angles across the lines. Since we had no birds in our apartment, I turned that project into a piggybank by closing the sides and leaving an opening on top. When I brought my project home, I asked Daddy to take a picture of it so that I could send it to my tía Isabel.

Not all letters from the family back in the old country contained good news. Sometimes, there were sad stories about people who had passed away, floods in various towns, or when the strong hurricane of 1978 destroyed most of Abuelo's farms and the big jabillo tree. The news about the jabillo tree made me very sorrowful. I felt a connection to the tree. I had very fond memories of my time spent reading, observing life from above, and napping up on top where three thick branches formed its comfortable landing. I wondered what the family would do for shade while they gathered on the side of the house to tell stories and have the afternoon coffee.

My older friend Elizabeth was a person I frequently wrote to after she moved to Ohio. She was my mother's friend who often talked to me about various social issues happening in New York City in the early seventies. Elizabeth once explained to me some of the reasons about the constant fires in the Bronx. I did not understand much of what she said but continued to think about the issue every time a new building went down in ashes. She would answer any questions without getting annoyed like most adults who I knew. She spoke proper English and Spanish and encouraged me to advance when I struggled with English pronunciation before I spoke the language fluently. Elizabeth wrote to me various times a year. I wrote my first English letter to her when I turned fourteen. The summer before I went away to college, while she was visiting her family in New

York, she came to see our family and gifted me a small statue of the Virgin Mary. Elizabeth said to always keep it near for protection and blessings. That little statue has taken a place on my nightstand for the rest of my life. I continue to pray daily for guidance and protection. These are virtues I have learned from various adults who have helped in shape my life.

During my years growing up, it was necessary to write letters to people. That was still the main mode of communication for most people. The letters to the homeland created a sense of connection and everlasting bonds with the members of the extended family. They remained in the homeland but continued to pay attention to us over the years. Their letters often displayed an abundance of love and good intentions. The family often asked about our well-being upon hearing the distressful news being generated in the media about life in the streets of New York in the 1970s. When my abuelo wrote, he often sent lengthy prayers of our safety. Tia Isabel always ended her letters with a phrase of blessings and protections. "Que Dios los bendiga y los proteja," she would write.

THE TRIP TO THE HOMELAND

The months prior to our second trip to the Dominican Republic, Tia Isabel continued to write about her excitement for our upcoming visit. Abuelo also wrote about his happiness about the trip. This time, he asked Tia Isabel to write the letter for him, and she included it in the same envelop with hers.

Over the time we spent in the new country, each one of us tried to make our family name proud. Our abuelo had commanded us to do so before we left the homeland in 1971. The Christmas during my junior year in high school, all six members of my family returned to the Dominican Republic for a visit. We had waited with excitement for a chance to return to visit our extended family. We arrived on Christmas day and remained for a week.

I remember Daddy's excitement to see Abuelo again. He could barely hold his joy and in often bursts of "Ay, mi viejo!" I watched Daddy rub his hands in excitement the same way he did when watching the Yankees ball games.

When we arrived at Abuelo's farm, we discovered that by then he was almost blind. He had lost most of his eyesight due to glaucoma complications and various strokes he had suffered after Abuela's passing five years before. Despite his ailments and that he walked slower, Abuelo continued to have energy for all types of activities. Abuelo was able to recognize each one of us and enjoyed listening to our stories about our new life in New York. He asked many questions and told us stories about the last hurricane and his farm.

"Quiero aprender a bailar música Disco," announced Abuelo soon after we arrived. He explained to us about his enthusiasm for learning to dance like John Travolta. Abuelo was a very good dancer even for an old man. He was born before the twentieth century. He loved dancing to all types of music and enjoyed parties. Abuelo never drank, nor smoked, but enjoyed having a good time. My sister Loli taught him how to disco dance before we returned to our home in New York, and Abuelo enjoyed his new steps and said he would now try to imitate the moves from the handsome young man in the movies.

In addition to changes in Abuelo's health, the rest of the extended family continued to move on. Several cousins had grown up and moved on to pursue their adult lives. Others had children of their own, and some had nice jobs with big companies or with government agencies. Several moved onto the capital city. Abuelo complained that the new generation was not interested in the farmland.

My aunt Isabel had taken the role as head of the family since my abuela passed away. She and her husband oversaw what remained of Abuelo's farmland and supervised his health and care. Their oldest daughter moved to Abuelo's house permanently, and she took care of him full time. Aunt Isabel continued to be sweet and caring. Upon passing by my side, she always gave me a kiss and a hug. She was the person most like my dad, as she showed lots of affection to all of us. The house she had begun to build upon our departure years ago had been finished. It was a large dwelling with a comfortable veranda in the back that was surrounded by fruit trees that provided lots of shade and the constant smell of flowers that was carried from across the farm in the back.

That week of our visit, we traveled throughout the southern coastline of the Dominican Republic. We went on a different excursion every day. At night, we went out to dine at restaurants and a couple of times, we went dancing with our cousins. The older cousins were impressed that we were still able to speak proper Spanish and dance to merengue. They assumed we had become too Americanized and had forgotten or abandoned our original cultural practices.

During our visit, we also spent a day at the beach. That was such a treat. I welcomed swimming in the warm and clear beach waters with the soft and light sand of the Caribbean Sea. I loved watching the brightly colored schools of fish passing by as I stood still in awe when they swoosh along to hide behind the shelter of the reef at a distance.

"Ay!" I screamed when a swordfish passed by my leg, but it ignored me as it chased some other creature in the water. Later, I wrote about my encounter with the swordfish and expressed admiration for its focus on what really mattered to it. I decided that I wanted to be like that swordfish swimming after its prey.

During our visit that holiday, my parents took me to visit universities in the Dominican Republic. They hoped that I would choose to attend college back in the homeland since they had heard that colleges were expensive in the United States. While visiting colleges there, I realized that I was already English dominant when academics was required. I was unfamiliar with academic words in Spanish and was not about to reverse my language learning again. Visions of 1971 came to my mind as we traveled across the island to visit the Universidad del Este, which was an American university in the Dominican Republic. While listening to the admissions counselor there, I quietly realized that I wanted to continue my pursuit to attend college in the United States. Later, I concluded that I was just like the swordfish. Like it, I also was laser focused on what personally mattered to me.

The sea breeze tickling my cheeks as we drove to the airport for our return trip to New York reminded me of the first time I left the homeland. During that time, an unknown world where my parents lived awaited my arrival. I was very young the first time and now was much closer to being an adult. The new land had provided opportunities to grow at a fast pace due to the many obstacles and hurdles placed along my path by the complex society where we lived. While deep in thought about my life ahead, "I will earn a scholarship and attend college in the United States," I told my parents when they asked me about my plans. They, in turn, did not say anything at that moment, but their sighs and rolling of the eyes indicated their disappointment about my decision.

Every time I return to the homeland, I immensely enjoy the quality time spent with my extended family. I also admire the hardships some of the family members have endured and overcome over the years. I have felt pride every time I discover a wonderful story about any of our ancestors. Such as when I visited the Museo de la Resistencia and read about my mother's older brother who was part of a student revolt against the dictator Trujillo in the 1950s and ended up as a political prisoner at that time. During my uncle's time as a political prisoner, he lost several fingers during the torture he endured. It was at that time that I understood my own feelings for rebellion and social justice. *It is in my blood*, I thought happily, upon reflecting about my uncle's struggles and resistance.

I value the warmth and love that the extended family continues to have for those of us who left many years ago. They remain in constant communication with us and enjoy celebrating with us whenever possible, as well as grieving along when sad times occur.

I have studied Dominican literature and culture at the college and graduate levels to feel more connected to my roots. During those studies, I have been able to sit with and interview great Dominican writers such as Pedro Mir and Bruno Rosario Candelier. Their writings have inspired thoughts of understanding, hope, and aspiration during my path as an educator. Pedro Mir shared how he wrote some of his best work hidden in an outhouse in fear that the spies for the dictator would discover that he was writing about sociopolitical abuse. My total admiration for his work goes beyond any words that I could ever utter, and I am always honored to have been able to meet someone of such caliber.

Over the years, I began to feel detached from having a life in my homeland, and unlike my sisters, I have never returned to make a living there. American soil is where I have chosen to be. Just around the time I was becoming an adult, I chose a life in the land where I was not welcomed many times. New York was the place where my parents had chosen to take me when I was about to be eleven years old and where my thoughts belonged now. "I am here to stay," I told my parents more than once.

# ALWAYS MOVING FORWARD

"This is where I belong now," I told myself around the time I had become an adult. Receiving a chance to study at a prestigious university with a scholarship kept me focused on my studies and allowed me to ignore the distractions I faced daily both at home, in school, and every other place I went.

The first days my siblings and I arrived in New York City in 1971, my parents made it clear to us that they had uprooted our family from our homeland so that we could have the opportunities that were denied to them due to life circumstances. "The United States of North America is the land of opportunity for all those who were willing to work hard and persevere," said my father throughout our formative years. He slowly spelled out the name of our new country each time he said it. Every chance he got to talk to us about life, Daddy would say this over and over as if to make a permanent imprint in our minds. He also used to say how because he didn't have the chance to get a college degree, he was now bound to the types of work he had been doing since the day after arriving to this country.

Daddy worked at various factories in the manufacturing field before those were taken out of New York and onto other states and other countries. He also cleaned floors as a janitor in various large buildings like the Museum of Natural History for a while and large churches around the city. As a supplement income, he sold home products from a catalogue even though his English was limited. He also managed a bodega when his friend retired, where he was exposed to violence and crime many times. Finally, Daddy had taught himself to be a handyman so he could take on the job of building superintendent, where he hoped to save some money since rent was included as part of his compensation for this job. As far as I can remember, Daddy always had more than one job. Sometimes Daddy worked three jobs so that we could be provided the necessary things to thrive in New York City. He worked day and night and still found time to come home to eat dinner with us most nights. Twice every baseball season, he went to see the Yankee game at the nearby stadium. He always managed to show joy, although deep inside, his body ached from lack of rest and exposure to the elements. "Trabajo por ustedes," he often said that he would work these jobs for as long as necessary so that his children would focus on their studies and never have to suffer the aches and insecurities of poverty as he had.

The more distractions I was exposed to, the more focused I remained to accomplish my goals of becoming my family's first college graduate. I was like the swordfish who swooshed by my side one time. Watching some of my classmates drop out of school or getting into trouble did not distract me from my plans. I was intentional about accomplishing all the goals I had set out for myself since I was very young. Sometimes, I modified those goals to fit various circumstances, which changed several of the paths I took in life. When my parents would not allow me to attend a specialized arts school, I decided to become the best I could be at the science-focused honors program in my high school. My objectives were always set with memories of my abuelo's voice saying, "Make our family name proud."

During my early years of schooling, I had received so many awards at the end of every grade that it became a laughing joke in my family that I needed to bring an empty suitcase to carry all the plaques and trophies I received each time. I remained committed to and competitive about most things I did. I purposefully wanted to be at the top of my class and worked hard to achieve among the top 5.

Although I was not valedictorian of my high school class, it gave me pleasure to know I ranked number 3 in a graduating class of about five hundred students. All top 5 students were just decimal points from each other when final averages were calculated.

My journal writing helped me understand issues and hurdles I encountered daily. There I wrote things that bothered me both at school and at home. As I wrote, many obscure issues were clarified over time. Although during my development as a young woman I did not understand many of the social ills I wrote about, I continued to search for answers to my questions and hoped that someday I could understand and accept life as it was presented to me.

Deep inside me, I wished that the types of ills I saw in the streets of the Bronx, would all eventually get solved by people who could make a positive impact. Later, I learned the types of issues that concerned me and some of the reasons for violence and poverty. I learned about racism and realized that I had lived it many times. Although my friends and I had grown up surrounded by violence and a harsh outside environment, there were many things we were not aware of as we searched for answers to life issues.

As I wrote in my journal, I remember feeling very down and pausing to pray to my abuela's spirit in heaven and my abuelo's thoughts and good energy to guide me. Writing in my journal was my refuge, my special space in this large society that I found hard to navigate.

By the time I was a senior in high school, my family moved to an apartment where I had my own little room. When I had to make a college decision, I decided to focus on my plans and to remain calm as I rejoiced in my accomplishment of getting accepted into every college for which I had completed applications. The day for decision-making came along. That day, I was already at my bedroom window when the first rays of sun appeared. Looking out in front, there was a big stone wall that separated the building next door, but from the space above, the sun rays were shining through my windowpanes. I was reading each acceptance letter again and trying to make sense of the financial packages I had been offered. I decided to proceed with my day and face my fears and aspirations, just like Abi had taught me years before.

Since I did not have anyone older at home nor at school to discuss my college choice decision, prior to decision day, I made a chart of the offers of scholarships and the expenses each school would require. Somehow, I figured out that my first school choice was not much more expensive than the rest of the other schools. A nice scholarship offer had been made to me. I wanted to go away to college, and I'd loved the Wellesley College campus when I visited during my junior year. Since that visit, they had sent me various letters of encouragement to apply. As the morning light came to full shine and the rest of the family began to wake up on that first day of spring holiday, I had already decided where I would attend college. "I am here to stay," I heard myself whisper to no one.

A NEW PATH

Reaching adulthood was a significant step in my life trajectory. By the time I turned eighteen, I was cognizant of the implications of reaching that milestone and the uncertainty and challenges that come with age. The butterflies in my stomach continued to make disruptions every time I thought about the next phase of my life.

High school graduation was most rewarding for me, and I think also for my close friends.

"We made it!" was a common phrase among us. We were all on our path to attend college. Some of my friends attended local colleges, and others went far away. As we all said our goodbyes, we knew that graduation day would be the last time many of us would see each other. We hugged each other constantly during those last days of high school. As we walked each other to the bus stop, we talked about our fears of our lives ahead. None of us knew what college life would be about since our parents did not attend college.

Although we all lived in the Bronx, the borough was very large, and many of us lived far away from each other. My dearest friend Narcy was attending a local college, and I knew I would continue to see her. My other good friend, Jackie, was going away to the same school I had chosen.

Many of us had earned full scholarships to prestigious schools. It was hard to decide what to do about many of the opportunities presented to us. "Do you think it'll be very hard to go away?" would say one of us. "I wonder what awaits us out there?" would interject the other. We often talked about our nerves and about being afraid of the unknown. Mostly, we discussed our feelings of being alone in this process.

When graduation day arrived, many of us joined in a group hug. One of our friends said a prayer as we hugged. I never again saw most of my high school friends. As scary as that was, off we went into the wide world of adulthood to continue to pave the way for our own lives.

The summer of 1979 was very busy and exciting. I worked full time at the local summer camp, and at the church of St. Andrew's rectory, where my mother worked on Saturdays. That church was located near the World Trade Center, the same set of building skeletons I had seen from a distance during my first visit to the Statue of Liberty close to nine years before. I used to walk around after work and admire the opulence of their height up close. Although very tall, I did not think they were as impressive aesthetically as other buildings in the city.

Part of what kept me busy that summer was preparing to go away to college. I made lists of paperwork I needed to complete before leaving for college. I made lists of materials and dorm items I needed to buy and bring with me. I made a list of the deadlines for several submissions I needed to make before leaving. Finally, I organized the paperwork at the local parish council, for which I was president, so that there would be a smooth transition when I left.

On Saturdays after work, in addition to walking around downtown Manhattan admiring the buildings and the complex narrow old city streets of the Iron and Financial districts, I also combed through nearby stores to purchase the items I needed and remain within my budget. And when the day arrived for departure to college, I had packed all my belongings in a small suitcase, a duffel bag, and a trunk.

At the end of that summer, there I was, eight years after arriving in this country as an immigrant, soon to be eleven-year-old girl from the Dominican Republic, reflecting on my parents' sacrifice to see that I would become the first college graduate in our family. The weight of such responsibility felt very heavy. My parents often reminded me of such honor, which I saw as a colossal challenge. I was attempting to navigate a world I did not know and had no footprint or trail to follow other than prayers and a huge sense of self-confidence. I had the confidence inherited from my abuelo Heriberto. I had the prayers gifted to me by both my abuelas, Arminda and Abi, and my hardworking, loving parents. My siblings, who were all younger, looked on and cheered me on every time I decided to move ahead. "Estamos todos en esto," would chime in my mother as she watched how happy they were for me and smiled to see us rejoicing together.

The days prior to my departure to college, there was a lot of commotion in our household. Although we were all tense at the idea that I would no longer be living at home, the love and caring expressed by each member of my family was something that eased the butterflies that constantly stirred my stomach.

It was a six-hour drive to Massachusetts, where my college was located. The drive there felt endless. Along the way, I was lost in thoughts as Daddy carried on conversations with the church friend who drove us there. Mami sat in the back seat with me and dozed off most of the way and cried whenever she was awake. She caressed my hair often and held my sweaty hand as well. When I was finally dropped off at my dorm and the car drove off, I felt as if I had a heavy load on my shoulders.

The entire ordeal of drop-off day at college has always been a blur in my mind. I guess the shock of feeling independent from my parents obscured my memory. The details of what that very first day on a college campus as a student signified to someone like me were all blurry for many years.

The morning after my arrival on campus seemed to be clearer when I tried to remember my new journey. I sat alone at the breakfast table and watched as other girls walked into the dining hall, waving and greeting each other. I felt alone although I was surrounded by many. I watched in silence. I hid my fear and uncertainty of the unknown with a smile. In my head, I prayed so that I might find a guide to help me with my ignorance as a college freshman.

By the time breakfast was over, I had placed my "fears into my pocket," as my abuela Abi often said. I moved along with the rest of the freshman girls to begin our college trek. Listening to them, I realized that they must have felt similar anxieties. This was the first full day of the rest of my journey as an adult in this new land that had finally begun to feel like home. It was September of 1979, and I had to make the effort to succeed and move ahead to honor my parents' efforts and to create a future for myself.

Angela M. Arias, EdD
Angelaarias646@gmail.com
New York
Summer 2022

Daddy and the four kids in the Dominican Republic - 1967

First grade photo Dominican Republic, 1966

Mami and Angel at the school gate 1972

Mami and I at 8th grade graduation

ABOUT THE AUTHOR

Dr. Angela Arias arrived in New York City at the age of ten with her three younger siblings after a few years of separation from her parents, who came from the Dominican Republic in search of better opportunities. She is a graduate of New York City public schools and attended Wellesley College on a scholarship. Upon receiving her bachelor's degree, she attended the State University of New York at Buffalo, where she received a master's degree. Dr. Arias obtained her doctorate in education from Walden University. She worked as a high school educator for thirty-four years before retiring in 2020. In her spare time, she mentors college and doctoral students to assist in their career and personal development. During the pandemic, she moved upstate New York to be close to her daughter, Elena. Dr. Arias enjoys reading, writing, cooking, and being close to nature.